THE PRIMARY SUBJECT MANAGER'S HANDBOOKS SERIES

Coordinating mathematics across the primary school

THE SUBJECT LEADER'S HANDBOOKS

Series Editor: Mike Harrison, Centre for Primary Education, School of Education, The University of Manchester, Oxford Road, Manchester, M13 9DP

To Hannah and Alice

Coordinating mathematics across the primary school

Tony Brown

UK	The Falmer Press, 1 Gunpowder Square, London, EC4A 3DE
USA	The Falmer Press, Taylor & Francis Inc., 1900 Frost Road, Suite 101, Bristol, PA 19007

First published in 1998

A catalogue record for this book is available from the British Library

ISBN 0 7507 0687 2 paper

Library of Congress Cataloging-in-Publication Data are available on request

Jacket design by Carla Turchini

Typeset in 10/14pt Melior and printed by Graphicraft Typesetters Ltd., Hong Kong

Contents

Part one
The role of the mathematics coordinator

Part two
What mathematics coordinators need to know

Part three
Whole school policies and schemes of work

Part four
Monitoring for quality

Part five
Resources for learning

List of figures

Acknowledgments

Many people have generously given me advice and encouragement in drawing this book together. I want to acknowledge the help I have received from Joanna Haynes for her intuitive grasp of what is important; Henry Liebling for his enthusiasm and insight; Ruth Merttens, Dick Tahta, and Nigel Williams for his inspiring teaching. Grateful thanks are also due to the many primary teachers who have shared their practice.

Series editor's preface

This book has been prepared for primary teachers charged with the responsibility of acting as subject managers of mathematics within their schools. It forms part a series of new publications that set out to advise such teachers on the complex issues of managing each element of the primary school curriculum.

Why is there a need for such a series? Most authorities recognise, after all, that the quality of the primary children's work and learning depends upon the skills of their class teacher, not in the structure of management systems, policy documents or the titles and job descriptions of staff. Many today recognise that school improvement equates directly to the improvement of teaching so surely all tasks, other than imparting subject knowledge, are merely a distraction for the committed primary teacher.

Nothing should take teachers away from their most important role, that is, serving the best interests of the class of children in their care and this book and the others in the series does not wish to diminish that mission. However, the increasing complexity of the primary curriculum and society's expanding expectations, makes it very difficult for the class teacher to keep up to date with every development. Within traditional subject areas there has been an explosion of knowledge and new fields introduced such as science, technology, design, problem solving and health education, not to mention the uses of computers. These are now considered entitlements for primary children. Furthermore, we now expect all children to succeed at these studies — not just the fortunate few. All this has overwhelmed a class teacher system largely unchanged since the inception of primary schools.

Primary class teachers cannot possibly be an expert in every aspect of the curriculum they are required to teach. To whom can they turn for help? It is unrealistic to assume that such support will be available from the headteacher whose responsibilities have grown ever wider since the 1988 Educational Reform Act. Constraints, including additional staff costs, and the loss of benefits from the strength and security of the class teacher system, militate against wholesale adoption of specialist or semi-specialist teaching. Help therefore has to come from exploiting the talents of teachers themselves, in a process of mutual support. Hence primary schools have chosen many and varied systems of consultancy or subject coordination which best suit the needs of their children and the current expertise of the staff.

In fact curriculum leadership functions in primary schools have increasingly been shared with class teachers through the policy of curriculum coordination for the past twenty years, especially to improve the consistency of work in language and mathematics. Since then each school has developed their own system and the series recognises that the one each reader is part of will be a compromise between the ideal and the possible. Campbell and Neill (1994) show that by 1991 nearly nine out of every ten primary class teachers had such responsibility and the average number of subjects each was between 1.5 and 2.2 (depending on the size of school).

These are the people for whom this series sets out to help to do this part of their work. The books each deal with specific issues whilst at the same time providing an overview of general themes in the management of the subject curriculum. The term *subject leader* is used in an inclusive sense and combines the two major roles that such teachers play when they have responsibility for subjects and aspects of the primary curriculum.

The books each deal with:

- *coordination*   a role which emphasises harmonising, bringing together, making links, establishing efficient routines and common practice; and,
- *subject leadership* a role which emphasises; providing information, offering expertise and direction, guiding the development of the subject, and raising standards.

The purpose of the series is to give practical guidance and support to teachers — in particular **what to do and how to do it**. They each offer help on the production, development and review of policies, and schemes of work; the organisation of resources, and developing strategies for improving the management of the subject curriculum.

Each book in the series contains material that subject managers will welcome and find useful in developing their subject expertise and in tackling problems of enthusing and motivating staff.

Tony Brown's book is designed as a resource to dip into. Although written primarily for teachers who are coordinators and subject leaders in mathematics, this book is a useful guide for anyone in the school who has a responsibility for the mathematics curriculum including the teacher with an overall role in co-ordinating the whole or key stage curriculum and, the deputy head and the head teacher.

In making the book easily readable Tony has drawn on his experience as a leader of courses for mathematics co-ordinators, as an OFSTED inspector and as someone who has been involved in mathematics education for a number of years.

Mike Harrison, Series Editor
January 1998

Introduction

This handbook for primary subject managers of mathematics is one of a series of new publications that tackle the complex issues of managing the primary school curriculum.

This handbook deals with specific issues whilst at the same time providing an overview of general themes in the management of the mathematics curriculum. The term *subject manager* is used in an inclusive sense and combines the two major roles that teachers play when they have responsibility for the mathematics curriculum. The handbook deals with:

■ *coordination*; a role which emphasises; harmonising, bringing together, making links, establishing efficient routines and common practice,

■ *subject leadership*; a role which emphasises; providing information, offering expertise and direction, guiding the development of the subject, raising standards.

The purpose of the handbook is to give practical guidance about supporting the mathematics curriculum: **what to do and how to do it**. It offers help on:

■ the production, development and review of policies, and schemes of work,

■ the organisation of resources,

■ developing strategies for improving the management of the mathematics curriculum,

■ supporting colleagues in the teaching of mathematics.

It is designed as a resource to dip into. Although written primarily for teachers who are coordinators and subject leaders in mathematics, this handbook is a useful guide for anyone in the school who has a responsibility for the mathematics curriculum, including the teacher with an overall role in curriculum coordination, the deputy head and the headteacher.

The handbook contains material that subject managers will welcome and find useful in developing their expertise and in tackling problems. It is divided into five parts.

1 The role of the subject manager
2 What the mathematics coordinator needs to know
3 Developing and maintaining policies and schemes of work
4 Monitoring to secure quality
5 Resources and contacts

Part one | The role of the mathematics coordinator

Chapter 1   The background

The subject leader's job has developed into a front-line post. Conferring subject responsibility on a single person has created a job of great importance in most schools. Twenty-five years ago the curriculum 'belonged' to the headteacher. Some headteachers chose to appoint maths coordinators, but many didn't. The coordinator's work was often quite different in both scope and depth from the work done today. Twenty five years ago a headteacher would be proud to talk about 'my' school. Everyone, including staff, parents, local authority advisers and HMI looked to the head to explain and discuss the school's curriculum, since it was the head, in most cases, who had chosen the content and form of the curriculum that teachers would follow. With relatively few externally imposed legal requirements, other than those relating to religious education, the headteacher was expected to have fashioned the curriculum from their own rich experience — and many of them did exactly that very successfully. In recent years the range and complexity of the curriculum has changed so dramatically that a single person cannot be expected to know in detail all the information that relates to all the subjects.

Until recently few children had the opportunity to study mathematics — the experience of most children in the 1950s and 1960s was of arithmetic. Few schools covered a broad science curriculum — nature study was the extent of scientific exploration for many children. RE seldom had a multicultural dimension. Design and technology, information technology, music and PE gave few opportunities for children to be creative and inventive. Children's experience of arithmetic seldom included opportunities for choice, decision making, invention or creativity. The assumptions inherent in the *using and applying* programme of study were seldom evident; although the original Nuffield teachers' books of the 1960s clearly show that some children were fortunate to experience mathematics as a creative and investigative activity that covered much more than arithmetic.

The curriculum no longer belongs to the headteacher. The head's role of determining the range and content of the curriculum, and their position as curriculum expert in every subject, has been replaced by a system with which we are still coming to terms; and which is continuing to develop and change. In most schools today, the subject leader has the responsibility of being the curriculum expert. Managing this role is an extraordinarily challenging task.

The demands of inspection

When the National Curriculum was imposed on schools, the curriculum became much more extensive, more detailed and more complex than teachers had previously experienced. Many schools moved quickly to appoint curriculum coordinators and to seek training for them. One of the most galvanising forces for change was the introduction of school inspection. In the brief time they are in school, inspectors need to discuss the mathematics curriculum in great detail. The demands of inspection have emphasised the need, wherever possible, for a single person within the school to speak authoritatively about the mathematics curriculum. The inspection process has been part of the driving force towards more elaborate and formal procedures for assessment, recording and reporting, and establishing the mathematics curriculum within whole school procedures. The effect of inspection has been to profoundly influence the nature and scope of the work of subject leaders who find themselves key players in the inspection process. The production of a school inspection report depends in no small measure on the subject leader and the way their role has been developed. They need the ability to prepare the ground well before the inspection. They need to be good communicators. They often have only a single interview during the inspection during which to communicate the school's strengths clearly and succinctly.

The inspection process has driven the development of the role of subject management in primary schools — and not always in a helpful way. School inspection has not been a very uplifting experience for the teaching profession in England. It is important to remind ourselves that the procedure in Wales differs from that in England and the experience of Welsh teachers does not entirely parallel that of their English colleagues. Inspection in Scotland is very different — no OFSTED — but a somewhat different inspection process involving HMI. One could speculate that after devolution in Scotland and following the introduction of a Welsh assembly, the teachers in England may find themselves the only group with a highly centralised, somewhat adversarial inspection process. There is a danger that the welter of national and LEA guidelines and instructions stimulated by these recent developments will smother creativity and invention completely. Their overall effect is an unnecessarily prescriptive and unrealistic series of demands.

Schools are the best places that our society has yet devised for the formal communication of social beliefs and ideals and for the transmission of the broad range of knowledge that we judge young people to need. There is an undeniable human dimension to schools that we ignore at our peril. This book seeks to address the human situation as an integral part of the process of schooling, and as an integral part of managing the mathematics curriculum.

The assessment and recording process has been badly managed by the various government quangos that have had involvement in it. Prior to the Dearing Review, many groups found the lack of clarity in the information to schools a useful way of putting pressure on teachers. The anti-teacher stance of several Secretaries of State encouraged this attitude. Teachers were allowed to interpret the legislation in a way that implied that everything a child did in maths had to be recorded. The Dearing Review clearly identified that the only legal requirement was to provide evidence at the end of each key stage. Government departments subsequently denied having implied anything else.

Teachers are still coming to terms with the complexities of the assessment process. There are important needs to be met within the school: to inform future planning; to monitor individual children's attainment; to assess equality of opportunity; to monitor the progress of the most and least able; to provide information to parents. It's helpful to make a distinction between assessment as a process of professional judgment and record-keeping, which is an administrative task. Many schools are still over-burdening themselves with record-keeping; either because they record too much trivial and unhelpful data, or, as is often the case, by collecting and recording the same information over and over again and reproducing it in different formats. Many schools need to review their record-keeping procedures to find ways of reducing the burden and making the process simpler and more efficient. As part of their review of record-keeping, coordinators need to ask themselves whether information is valuable: i.e. will it lead to improved standards, is it legally required, has it been recorded before, why is it being collected and produced, is there any information that we need and which we haven't got?

There are a number of national developments that are likely to have a major impact on the mathematics curriculum in the near future. Two in particular are likely to prove very influential. The first is the establishment of Numeracy Centres and the other is the almost inevitable emergence of a national training and qualification procedure for subject leaders. The curriculum currently provided by the Numeracy Centres requires a comparatively large amount of teaching time — an hour a day — and includes a high degree of prescription about how to teach the mathematics it contains. The new government is just as likely to adopt it as was its predecessor. If a 'numeracy curriculum' becomes a required part of a new National Curriculum then there will inevitably be intense pressure on the rest of the subjects taught in schools. At worst, Key Stage 1 will become a philistine 3Rs curriculum.

Draft proposals for training subject leaders and providing successful trainees with national qualifications were published late in 1996 by the Teacher Training Agency. The future of this quango is not particularly secure and its absorption into a General Teaching Council remains a possibility in the medium term. The draft proposals make some unrealistic demands on subject leaders, particularly when one reminds oneself that many people who are responsible for mathematics carry out the role unpaid, untrained and as an act of goodwill to the school.

The Cockcroft Report, published in 1982, provided a forward looking description of the work that a mathematics coordinator might be expected to do.

 In our view it should be part of the duties of the mathematics coordinator to:

- *prepare a scheme of work for the school in consultation with the headteacher and staff and, where possible, with schools from which the children come and to which they go . . .;*
- *provide guidance and support to other members of staff in implementing the scheme of work . . .;*
- *organise and be responsible for procuring . . . the necessary teaching resources for mathematics, maintain an up-to-date inventory and ensure that members of staff are aware of how to use the resources . . .;*
- *monitor work in mathematics throughout the school, including methods of assessment and record-keeping;*
- *assist with the diagnosis of children's learning difficulties and with their remediation;*
- *arrange school based inservice training for members of staff as appropriate;*
- *maintain liaison with schools from which children come and to which they go, and also with LEA advisory staff.*

(Cockcroft, 1982, para 355)

Becoming a subject leader can be regarded as having three stages; getting started, becoming established, being experienced. Although some subject leaders find themselves under pressure to do everything at once, there are some aspects of the role that are more realistically tackled at one stage rather than another. The next chapter looks at the three stages separately, but without losing sight of the whole picture.

Chapter 2

Three broad stages of role development

The three stages that are discussed here are:
1 Beginning as a coordinator.
2 Becoming established.
3 Being experienced — working on long-term projects.

Beginning

How well do you know the school? When you start out as a coordinator in your new job what you know about the school is very important. Getting promotion within your current school will feel very different from being appointed to a new school. These situations can give rise to very different demands. There are advantages in being able to say, 'I'm new round here. Tell me how you do . . .'. The opportunity doesn't last long and it's a useful strategy which can work for a few weeks.

For the person who is promoted from within their school, there are lots of advantages that come from having insider knowledge. However, we all have our blind spots. Being well acquainted with the school might mean that it is difficult to see alternative ways of doing things. You may have been appointed with a brief to institute change and this can prove more difficult for someone already in the school than for a new arrival. If you change roles within a school some colleagues may see you in a new light and treat you very differently from before, others may not treat you differently at all, despite your changed responsibilities. This range of responses can be disconcerting. Also, in practice it can very difficult to give up some of the responsibilities you thought you would be shedding in order to take on responsibility for mathematics.

If you've recently started a new job, take a few minutes to write down a list of things you miss from your old job and a list of things you are enjoying about the new one. How can you maximise the advantages of the new situation? How can you minimise the disadvantages? Put the list away and look at it again after a term or two. Were there things that you needlessly worried about? How did you manage to make the most of your move?

You may have taken a post in a new school or changed roles in your old school. Some things can be done straight away and it can be an advantage to get on with them immediately. Starting some things too soon can be a disadvantage. It can be useful to look at where to begin and what things to avoid doing too soon.

	Things I could do	Things to avoid doing
Advantages		
Disadvantages		

Negotiating your role when taking up a new appointment

If you are being interviewed for a coordinator's post, think about what you would need in terms of support if appointed, and negotiate for these opportunities at interview. You may be keen to get the job — but remember they'll be getting a highly qualified person with skills in a core subject. The deal works two ways and both sides have something to gain; and something to lose, if the negotiations aren't carried out carefully and in a way that satisfies everyone.

We all carry enormous numbers of assumptions around with us. When it comes to job interviews and appointments, it is best not to leave too many things as taken-for-granted. Don't assume that everyone is in agreement about what is meant by the questions and the answers during the interview. Instead, summon up courage and:

1 Be prepared to question people but first ask yourself about the assumptions that you and they are making, then voice them to see if there are assumptions being made that could lead to difficulties later.

2 Speak up about your assumptions, and what you need to have clarified as you tackle the questions. Make up your mind whether you want the job and say no if it doesn't feel right. If you're good enough to be short-listed then it'll happen again.

Job descriptions

What is most helpful is a job description which:
- is negotiated,
- defines the current role within realistic limits,
- contains agreed targets within agreed time periods,
- includes an effective appraisal process,
- contains advice on how to develop,
- identifies colleagues who the SMT (Senior Management Team) expect to collaborate with and support the coordinator over specific aspects of the work,
- allocates resources (e.g. classroom release time) that will be mobilised to make the tasks achievable,
- identifies some agreed outcomes (e.g. there will be a brief policy statement of approx. 2000 words, based on current practice and agreed by all members of staff).

You will need to see a copy of the job description that accompanies the post. If there isn't one, then ask to see the current one for the previous incumbent. Establish how job descriptions are drawn up: are they negotiated or handed down?

Coordinators' responsibilities should not be a limitless list of aspirations. Responsibilities should be well defined, and should make clear what the limits of responsibility are, as well as what resources are available to ensure that you can meet your responsibilities. For example, it is not acceptable to require you to monitor the teaching of mathematics without including guidance about how you are to do it. Some responsibilities have to be resourced. For you to carry out the work, there has to be provision made in terms of time, money, support and guidance, so that targets are realistic and achievable.

In some cases the actual detail will not appear on the written job description but will be part of the discussion you have with the head and SMT about how you will carry out the responsibilities. It is not acceptable for people to imply that since you have been given overall responsibility for mathematics you are responsible if anything goes wrong. The guidance, support and management of coordinators is the head's responsibility. Most headteachers recognise this and take a pride in ensuring that coordinators have all the support needed to work effectively. A good job description helps the coordinator feel supported, guided, protected, and liberated: able to use their own creativity to develop the job in their own way and find their own solutions to challenges within the agreed framework. What do job descriptions look like? They can vary widely in detail, style and layout. An example appears (Figure 2.1), with just the sections relating to mathematics reproduced.

Your role as maths coordinator

Developing your classroom practice: settling in

For all coordinators, irrespective of how they come to be in post, there is a need to:

■ become established as a respected class teacher of mathematics;

NAME _____

This document outlines the responsibilities of your work at the school and is divided into three parts.

1   The duties you are to carry out as a school teacher as set out in the relevant sections of the Pay and Conditions documents that currently apply.
2   Conditions of employment in relation to the management of our school.
3   Your responsibilities as subject leader in mathematics having been jointly agreed following negotiation.

3. Mathematics

You will share the overall management of the subject with the headteacher. Certain aspects of the role are delegated to you. You will liaise with the head regularly in order to ensure effective communication is maintained. In particular your responsibilities are:

To review, at the time identified in the SDP, the current policy and scheme of work in relation to the requirements of the National Curriculum and the needs of the school.

Release time from class responsibility for this aspect of the role to be negotiated and included in the SDP.

To maintain an overview of the mathematics curriculum throughout the school through discussions with SMT, colleagues, attendance at meetings and informal contacts.

To have access to the planning completed by all members of staff and to review them regularly to ensure there is progression and continuity in planning and evaluation of the mathematics teaching throughout the school.

To act as subject leader and give guidance to relevant members of staff to: support the development of the Early Years curriculum: support the development of the curriculum at both key stages.

To monitor the effective teaching of mathematics throughout the school. The focus of this work to be identified in the SDP and more precisely determined in consultation with SMT. Classroom release time: one half day per fortnight.

To liaise with the SENCO on issues relating to special needs and mathematics.

To assist newly qualified and newly appointed staff as required.

To advise staff about SATs and to give guidance about appropriate preparation of children.

To lead members of staff in inservice training in mathematics. This to be carried out informally at mutually arranged times and formally on day closures, staff meetings and other times as agreed.

To have the entitlement to appropriate inservice training and support as agreed with the head and SMT and within the SDP.

To advise staff on Health and Safety issues in the area of mathematics.

To maintain the list of resources and equipment for mathematics annually and to ensure this is available to members of staff.

To advise the headteacher of future budget requirements to maintain and develop the human and physical resourcing of mathematics.

To be responsible for managing the resource budget for mathematics in collaboration with the head.

To post information on courses and other opportunities for staff development in mathematics.

To remain informed of local and national issues and to keep abreast of current developments in the subject.

Signed _____ Headteacher. Signed _____ Subject leader. Date: _____

FIG 2.1
Job description — proforma

- acknowledge the range of experience and expertise among your colleagues;
- get to know what mathematics is actually being taught to children and what the practice is like through the school;
- negotiate a timetable for establishing some realistic personal targets: for the first few weeks, over the next term, through your first year, including how your work as a coordinator will be reviewed and appraised;
- recognise how to act so that you can protect both yourself and others from unrealistic demands and the very damaging effects of stress.

Using outside agencies to support you when you get started

After your appointment as a coordinator it is worth arranging to meet LEA advisory staff and freelance subject consultants, and to consider attending a course. An advisory teacher or visiting consultant can be bought in to meet you and discuss your new role. They can observe you teach, work with a group of children alongside you or take a demonstration lesson on an area of mathematics that you want to focus on. They can discuss ways to review your planning, or your teaching, and help you find ways of developing an area like *using and applying*. They can help you with methods of informal and formal assessment of children, help you develop criteria and the necessary skills for the assessment of children's work and provide a pre-inspection check for you. Although it costs money to bring in specialist help, it is a cost-effective way of improving the mathematics curriculum in a school. Many schools buy in services and these may include a proportion for induction of new staff. It's always important to negotiate at interview and to indicate what you think is an appropriate level of support for you as a newly appointed subject leader.

The experience of working alongside a subject specialist provides experiences that you can call on when you begin working alongside colleagues. Sharing your class can give you opportunities to examine chosen aspects of your teaching. A consultant can offer you ideas that can in turn be offered to colleagues after you have developed them with your own class. This can become a model of inservice support that eventually develops throughout the school.

You could buy two half day visits at the beginning and end of your first term. Many outside specialists will already know the school and be familiar with its strengths and weaknesses. They may have valuable professional information to pass on. Between visits you can work with the SMT to draw up a list of targets and begin work on some of them. A second meeting with a specialist would allow a review of your settling-in period and some advice about the next steps to be taken.

Thinking yourself into a leadership role

However skilled we are at working with children, when we take on a role that explicitly includes the professional development of colleagues, many of us find it challenging and we may feel de-skilled for a while. 'What can I offer them?' is a nagging question that often emerges. It's worth reminding ourselves that many of the skills needed for successful classroom lessons with children are the same as those needed to provide good quality professional development for colleagues.

Teachers teach in different ways and a degree of tolerance is needed when we meet people whose methods seem very different from our own. If you are working with them try to leave your 'baggage' at the door of their classroom. If there are any changes to make in the way they teach, then it will be *they* who make them and from where they are in their professional practice. An effective role for the coordinator is to help colleagues focus on something very specific, and to generate questions that raise the quality of discussions about curriculum development.

The coordinator has to find a style of curriculum leadership that enables a group of people who work very differently to develop and explore new ideas together. The ways in which we work and our level of effectiveness vary with our feelings of confidence. When we are self confident we can more easily engage with what others say without feeling that they are somehow getting at us. Establishing confidence in our ability to do a new job is very important — not just because we feel better but because we are also much more effective and open to others. An important start to the new job **is to learn to listen to what other people are *actually* saying, rather than trying to hear what we want to hear**.

Some things to consider:
- It's easier to work with a clear brief from the SMT (this is not the same as a narrow or prescriptive set of instructions). What are the expectations of the SMT: are they being realistic and have you been provided with the resources to tackle the work they want you to do?
- Ask colleagues what *they* want and need (and recognise that some will say, 'To be left alone.').
- Tell colleagues what you believe in and what you hope to do. Ask their opinion about a wide range of issues.
- Don't hide your idealism, but be prepared to be thought naive.
- Learn how to listen without always commenting or having a ready answer.
- Avoid being bounced into making decisions you're not ready to make. Some people will ask you for advice when you're just about to start a lesson. When asked, 'Have you got a minute?', you can put the decision back with the questioner: 'I can only give you a minute now, but I can give you ten minutes at break time. What's best for you?'
- Develop phrases for postponing decisions, and use them when you haven't had time to think through the consequences; e.g. 'Could you drop me a note about that?' 'I need to sleep on that.' 'I need to hear some other peoples' views before I can give you an answer.'
- Approaching the long-serving member of staff can be daunting. Remember though — most people want you to succeed because these days schools have to work as a close knit team to be successful. The school's success depends on the success of every individual. A long-serving colleague will have enormous experience. Ask them for advice. Talk to them about the techniques they employ in solving organisational and other challenges. Don't patronise, copy or reject — just ask and you'll probably get good advice.
- Everyone needs to feel valued so make a habit of asking advice of everyone from the most to the least experienced. Give them genuine problems that you are wrestling with; e.g. managing a difficult parent, coping with a problem child, gathering ideas for the use of some apparatus. This gets

people talking about the problems of teaching mathematics and helps destroy the idea that your appointment as coordinator means you know it all.

- However much you try, some colleagues may well try to manoeuvre you into the role of 'Super-Teacher'. Stay well clear.

Becoming established and managing change

As you become established you are likely to be involved in a wide range of activities including; reviewing policy statements, auditing resources, monitoring the coverage of the National Curriculum throughout the school. You will probably need to review a great many things, including: current planning, assessment procedures, existing schemes of work, the use of resources including commercial scheme material. This may be a good time to begin working with colleagues in their classrooms. Agree a focus beforehand, e.g. looking at how a small group of children can demonstrate mathematical reasoning. Then agree on what the outcomes will be. Who will be included in discussions of what went on in the classroom? If colleagues are unused to being observed, it's much better to make the children's mathematical activity the focus of any observations.

Effective development of the mathematics curriculum depends on your ability to integrate these various tasks. Without a sense of purpose, the whole process can feel like tinkering. It cannot be overemphasised that a sense of purpose should emerge from an increasingly articulate description of current practice throughout the whole school. Teachers have different strengths, and descriptions of current practice need to include the variations that will always exist when teachers work together.

The tasks, the reviews, the discussions and the document writing should flow from the process of describing and accounting for current practice. This will eventually lead on to an explanation and evaluation of current practice and from this you will be able to articulate the next stage, an appropriate development process that matches the needs of

> ...change, — constant, accelerating, ubiquitous — is the most striking characteristic of the world we live in and ...our educational system has not yet recognised this fact.
>
> (Postman and Weingartner, 1973, p. 13)

your unique situation and one that will improve and enrich the mathematics curriculum in your school.

It can take a long while to settle into a new role. There is a lot of pressure to get things done quickly, but this doesn't necessarily ensure the right things get done. An impending inspection can drive colleagues to make unrealistic demands and create a climate of panic with little being produced that is of high quality. Many senior managers in school still believe that 'everything has to be written down to show the inspectors when they arrive.' This is not always realistic and sometimes it can actually damage a school's credibility. What inspectors are looking for in terms of paperwork is evidence that the curriculum is being **managed** and is moving in a direction that will lead to improvement — particularly in children's attainment. Take a few minutes to write down how you are managing the various parts of your job.

'May you live in interesting times,' is reputedly an old Chinese curse. In recent years the pace of change has accelerated. Managing rapid change has become a major part of many peoples' lives, both in and out of education.

The job of curriculum development never stops. Efficient and effective management of the curriculum is all that can reasonably be asked of schools and teachers. Colleagues retire, newly qualified staff arrive, job responsibilities change, new resources are bought, new practices emerge. All is flux: nothing remains the same. Effective management of the changing curriculum is the effective and, hopefully, comfortable management of change itself. Effective coordinators have a finger on the pulse. They can describe the present situation and can demonstrate that, increasingly, changes to the curriculum have been planned for in advance.

Becoming established without being overwhelmed requires skilful means. Being given unrealistic targets (e.g. 'Get the new scheme of work written by the end of next term') can be a clear sign of the stress that members of the SMT are under. Unrealistic demands have to be gently but firmly resisted if you are to do more than just survive. When a colleague is suffering from stress, their stress can easily

Within each broad area identify one or two precise things to focus on	Write down what you actually do. Look at current planning, current practice and current provision
Monitoring the curriculum	What do you do to keep yourself informed?
Managing the curriculum	How do you help colleagues to maintain and follow agreed procedures relating to; current planning, current practice and current provision?
Managing the paperwork	Can you identify where the gaps are? Have you got a plan to manage anomalies? Does the paperwork describe and match current practice? Does the paperwork look neat and presentable?
Managing the budget and prioritising expenditure	How are current levels of equipment and resources maintained? How do you prioritise staff development and support for colleagues?
Setting realistic targets	How do you set targets for the term, the year, the next three years? How do you do this for yourself? How do you help individual colleagues and teams?

FIG 2.2
Managing the coordinator's role

spread throughout all the staff. It is in your interests to avoid succumbing too. The most effective way to survive is to be firm about negotiating realistic tasks and timetables from the outset. Many people are afraid to. They fear the disapproval of colleagues that they imagine will follow every attempt to refuse to take on unrealistic burdens. The danger is unhappiness and ill health. It is essential that we all learn how to say 'No,' skilfully while continuing to show care and understanding for the other people involved. There are several ways to reduce the risk of stress and one of the first things to check is whether you're causing your own problems by being too eager to take on more work. If you're in the habit of inviting extra work, then you have to deal with your own habitual behaviour. Assuming that this is not the case, then one way to manage requests for extra work is to take a rational stance. If the request comes from a senior colleague then you can ask them to be responsible for the rescheduling of priorities that will allow it to be done.

- I can do x but I'll have to drop something else — what do you suggest gets postponed?
- I can't do x until I've completed y — unless you want me to leave y for a while.
- If I take on x I'll need w weeks in which to do it. If you want it done quicker then someone will have to help me. Who do you suggest?

> Guy Claxton writes in his constructive and sensitive book on managing change and stress in teaching: 'Often, teachers will be working for change in an ethos that does not support them in their intention. Part of their job must therefore involve working to create a more supportive atmosphere for themselves...'
> (1989, p. 131)

Settling in to the job

What signs have you noticed that suggest you're beginning to settle in and are being accepted as established? How effectively do you use the opportunities that occur? (see Figure 2.3)

You may need to look at your current situation in more depth. The following checklist (Figure 2.4) is quite specific and should help you to be more precise in pinpointing

FIG 2.3
Judging your success at establishing
yourself in the role

Signs that suggest you've become established	How did you respond?
Colleagues start to come for advice.	
Someone enthusiastically shows you some children's work.	
A local adviser comes in to pick your brains.	
Colleagues confidently challenge your opinion.	

FIG 2.4
Areas of increasing effectiveness

Areas of increasing effectiveness	Tick
Providing a good model of mathematics teaching in your classroom.	
Establishing a good working relationship with colleagues and children.	
You are confident despite not knowing the answer to every question that colleagues pose. Colleagues have respect for your efforts and your integrity.	
Colleagues are following the curriculum plan with increased confidence. They use the planning and the resources effectively.	
You have put in place sufficient support and guidance to allow individual colleagues to develop an individual style and approach.	
Most colleagues are open to your ideas about how to improve teaching and learning.	
You are working towards providing comprehensive support and guidance for; curriculum planning, implementation and evaluation, curriculum monitoring, children's assessment, recording and reporting.	

© Falmer Press Ltd

where you are being effective. You can put a tick against the areas you are covering and then make some notes to show exactly how you are achieving your targets.

Responsibility for the mathematics curriculum is often diffuse and can overlap with other responsibilities. It's useful to identify who is responsible for the various elements of the work of coordination. Discussion and negotiation will provide a clearer picture of who is responsible for what. Developing your own version of the grid below can help you identify the range of responsibilities (Figure 2.5). It might be useful to devise a grid like this with colleagues during part of a staff meeting.

Effortless effort — managing subtle change

Many developments stand the best chance of success when you are well established. A higher level of trust and confidence is needed for initiating and supporting changes to teaching than to changes in planning. At the moment, change is being driven predominantly by external demands. These

Developments to be tackled	Major responsibilities					
	Coordinator	SMT	Head	All staff	Others in school	Outside agencies
Classroom practice						
Curriculum leadership						
Auditing the maths curriculum						
Negotiating realistic targets for development						
Managing SEN and able pupils						
Drawing up targets for the SDP						
Developing base-line assessment and assessment at Y4						
Monitoring SATs						

FIG 2.5
Identifying the range of responsibilities

often have contradictory elements and this fact can lead to feelings of frustration and confusion within the school team. Statements from different external groups may include, for example; demands to 'go back to basics' and concentrate on the core subjects, to abandon group work, to get children to be more socially aware and responsible, to teach mainly arithmetic, to copy teaching styles lifted wholesale out of very different cultures, to prepare children for the future world by covering the full ten subject curriculum.

One major purpose of schooling is to maximise the children's academic attainment. The key factor that influences attainment is the quality of the teaching. What ultimately determines the quality of education in school is the skill, knowledge and expertise of teachers. Improving what is available to children in the classroom can only be achieved when teachers look critically at their own practice, find ways to develop their art, have the support and respect of parents, politicians and others, and have resources that are appropriate for what is asked of them. Resources are finite and that means difficult choices have to be made so that the best course of action can be found for the circumstances that prevail. The coordinator's role is crucial in supporting improvements in the quality of teaching and learning. For example, teachers need subtle support when:

- it is evident that children in some classrooms are not making sufficient progress, given what is known of their capability,
- teachers want to extend their skills by incorporating teaching styles and methods that are new and unfamiliar to them,
- resources are not being used effectively,
- the school needs to make sophisticated modifications to the curriculum in the light of inspection findings or other experience.

Here are seven ways in which we can collect information that can help us build a picture of what is happening through the school.
1 Talking to colleagues informally, and giving advice;
2 Keeping a notebook of thoughts, ideas and the results of discussions;

3 Making a regular habit of looking at all the medium-term and short-term planning that colleagues are producing;

4 Getting a small amount of time to visit classrooms to work or observe colleagues as they teach;

5 Being given samples of children's work from colleagues from across the school on a regular (but not necessarily frequent) basis;

6 Walking through the entire school (possibly with the whole staff) on a regular basis to look at displays in classrooms and corridors;

7 Reading lesson evaluations that are part of the daily or weekly planning sheets, to see how colleagues are evaluating their mathematics teaching.

The history of curriculum development is littered with proud failures. Many projects absorbed years of effort and some cost millions of pounds. Those that failed, did so by and large, because they were planned as something to be *done to schools* and teachers were not part of the decision-making process from the outset. What is crucial is to secure agreement and a genuine commitment to planned change. What is true for big projects is also true for ensuring successful change within a single school. The best conditions for success are created when colleagues:

■ know you very well, are comfortable with you and trust your judgment;

■ feel ready for the planned changes;

■ know that their views and ideas count and that the whole team is working together.

When advocating change, it's useful to consider what people are being asked to give up as well as what they are being asked to take on. For some, a change of practice (e.g. increasing the amount of whole class teaching) may be accomplished easily, whilst for other teachers in the school the change to a newly agreed practice can mean an immense upheaval, the replacement of familiar classroom practices with something that feels very uncomfortable. An experienced coordinator plays a key role in creating the climate for a healthy attitude towards tackling the unfamiliar.

On their own, externally generated rules, directives, instructions and guidance are not usually sufficiently subtle to make things better. They need to be interpreted and modified to fit particular schools. Especially in the case of mathematics, the experienced coordinator is quite often the only person who has the range of skills and knowledge required to implement long-lasting improvements to the curriculum. When curriculum change is at its most effective it feels natural, exciting and something to learn from. It becomes effortless effort.

Some ways to review your role

There are a number of ways in which coordinators find their role being reviewed. Some methods are formal while others are quite informal. It's sometimes difficult to keep yourself aware of how you are growing into the role. Our knowledge, skills and insights are developing all the time but we are not always conscious of our professional growth.

Coordinators need a meta-awareness: being aware of changes in their own behaviour in response to the demands of the job. One aspect of the role is to monitor and support professional development in colleagues. This is made easier if coordinators are aware of their own growth (Figure 2.6). It is important to be able to keep track of what is happening to you as the job unrolls. Keeping informal notes of your own professional growth can be a particularly helpful way of doing this. Making notes focuses the attention since notes have to be selective. Those who are natural keepers of diaries have a relatively easy method open to them. Diaries provide a rich source of material to look back over. Other people may need to find another method that will provide opportunities to record what they notice. Try writing a note to yourself beside each of the three statements below:

FIG 2.6
Recording your personal
development in role

	The situation	Why it's important to you
Describe something that's been really successful recently		
Describe something or someone that you are avoiding		
Describe something you've tried that's left you feeling disappointed.		

What sort of things have turned out to be successful, easy, difficult, avoidable?

Trying to take a detached view for a moment, are there any patterns in your behaviour that stand out?

- Are you aware how colleagues feel when they are talking to you about mathematics?
- Are you comfortable with the idea that some colleagues may see you as the 'expert'?
- Is it difficult to get a clear picture of what's going on because you can't get some of the information you need?
- Is everyone in your school clear about your role?
- What ambiguous or contradictory aspects to your role can you identify?
- What types of situation leave you feeling skilled, de-skilled, happy, threatened, confident, unconfident?
- Does working with some colleagues leave you feeling confident, do others leave you feeling deskilled?

Make a note of your answers to each of these questions. Jot down any other observations you've made about your role and the way it's developing and changing. Find someone to talk to about what you notice. What is significant for you? What patterns have emerged? Do you sometimes get stuck because you only have one way of doing things? Can you talk to someone about finding an alternative approach? Do other coordinators who you know have ways of managing their work that you could try out in your situation?

Binds and overload

These are a feature of all teaching roles. The causes are worth looking at because some are self-inflicted and we can free ourselves from some of them. There are several reasons why the job of coordinator can easily reach overload: there are also several possible consequences. For example, feeling guilty is a major problem for many teachers. Feeling guilty about not feeling well and therefore not being able to 'do our best' is possibly one of the most miserable binds in which we can put ourselves.

R D Laing recognised the binds we create for ourselves in our lives. It's helpful to look at them, recognise aspects of ourselves and our professional work and explore ways of breaking some of the binds that we use on ourselves and others.

> JILL   You think I'm stupid
> JACK   I don't think you're stupid
> JILL   I must be stupid to think you think I'm
>   stupid if you don't: or you must be lying.
>   I am stupid every way:
>   to think I'm stupid, if I am stupid
>   to think I'm stupid, if I'm not stupid
>   to think you think I'm stupid, if you don't
>
> (Laing, 1972, p. 22)

And Laing cleverly captures a perennial problem faced by teachers, especially when they find themselves, or place themselves, in the role of the expert.

> There is something I don't know
>   that I am supposed to know.
> I don't know *what* it is I don't know,
>   and yet I am supposed to know,

and I feel I look stupid
    if I seem both not to know it
        and not know *what* it is I don't know.
Therefore I pretend I know it.
    This is nerve-racking
    since I don't know what I must pretend to know.
Therefore I pretend to know everything.

I feel you know what I am supposed to know
but you can't tell me what it is
because you don't know that I don't know what it is.

You may know what I don't know, but not
        that I don't know it,
and I can't tell you. So you will have to tell me everything.

(Laing, 1972, p. 56)

Perhaps it's worth reminding ourselves that teaching in primary schools is a good example of a 'Mission Impossible'. It is impossible, for example, to reach a point where the needs of individual children are completely met. Coordinators already have an impossible job as a class teacher. Some overload can be reduced by inventing or sharing simple ideas which help with day-to-day jobs like keeping track of resources, communicating important messages to colleagues or recording important information.

Delegating is a useful strategy that is all too frequently under-used in schools. Teachers often fear that delegation is just another word for imposition. However, it's worth asking others for help with tasks. Although a coordinator might hesitate to ask for help because everyone else seems very busy, colleagues will very often respond positively to a request because:

- they are pleased to help, and helping you now might make it easier for them to ask you for help another time;
- they see an opportunity for improving their own knowledge and understanding while not having to take full responsibility;
- they may want to 'try out' responsibility for another subject, to see what it feels like.

Where schools have given each core subject coordinator a 'shadow', the shadow-person (perhaps a Newly Qualified

Teacher (NQT) or recent returnee) can get some valuable experience from carrying out tasks delegated by the coordinator. Delegation isn't only a process of lightening the load, it can be beneficial to both parties and can be a useful form of staff development.

Being overloaded when you feel confident that you're doing a good job brings feelings and responses that are quite different from those experienced when you lack confidence or are the focus of criticism. The source of criticism can be someone else's panic attack! When we are feeling confident, many of us make lists and try to prioritise. Working down a list and ticking things off as we go is often therapeutic in itself. When we're in the middle of a panic, being told to make a list may not be the bit of advice we want to hear.

On balance it's often more effective to admit to being in crisis than to deny or hide it. Anxieties about loss of face are less damaging than the stress of pretending everything's all right. And appeals for sympathy and help are often heeded. When we are overloaded we may well stop monitoring those aspects of our behaviour that we usually manage automatically. We mislay essential pieces of paper and forget to make important phone calls. We drive badly and aren't very pleasant to other people. Often we simply don't notice what we're doing and how we're behaving, and this can have a knock-on effect on a situation that is already problematic. When suffering from stress, our blindness to what we are actually doing can reduce our effectiveness even further.

One advantage of having too much to do and being happy with the situation is that there's plenty of choice. Once we've acknowledged to ourselves and made it clear to others that we can't do all that's being asked, then there is some prioritising to be done. When we are prioritising we might as well choose to put something we like doing near the top of the list!

Part two

What mathematics coordinators need to know

Chapter 3   Managing the curriculum content

The Dearing Report published in 1994 contained recommendations about the amount of time to be spent teaching mathematics. Dearing suggested that at Key Stage 1 and at Key Stage 2, 126 hours per year need to be spent on maths. This is about 3.5 hours per week. This may represent a larger proportion of the curriculum for children in Key Stage 1 because in many schools the school day is shorter than at Key Stage 2. In theory a school has 20 per cent of its time available in addition to the National Curriculum. There is still a wide variation in the time spent on maths by different schools. What is less easy to support are variations between classes in the same Key Stage of a school.

The establishment of Numeracy Centres following Gillian Shepherd's initiative at the beginning of 1996 has led to a number of LEAs and schools trialling a very prescriptive programme that currently demands about five hours a week to be devoted exclusively to numeracy. Under current arrangements this could result in between six and eight hours per week to be devoted to the mathematics curriculum as a whole. Few schools could do this easily without disruption to the rest of the curriculum. Many teachers and LEA advisers are enthusiastic about the results achieved so far. Even after only a few months, there are reports that children are showing clear signs of increased numeracy skills.

After the last National Curriculum revision, schools were promised a five year moratorium on changes to the content. At the SCAA conference in June 1997 Estelle Morris, the minister for schools, promised a 'broad, enlightened' curriculum and no back-to-basics crusade. She did call for literacy and numeracy hours in every classroom but without breaking the Dearing embargo. The highly detailed content of the Numeracy Centre programme for schools will have to be assimilated by other schools, but the Numeracy Centre curriculum is likely to be required quite soon and 'Numeracy Hour' is the kind of sound bite beloved of politicians today.

The current Numeracy Centre programme spells out how teachers should present the mathematics and what teaching methods they should adopt. I have some sympathy with this approach. As I argue elsewhere (Brown and Merttens, in Merttens, 1997, pp. 77–98), there are many schools where very little 'active teaching' takes place and children receive very little direct input from teachers. There is no doubt that this is unsatisfactory and leaves children poorly equipped mathematically. The prescriptive nature of the numeracy programme is an attempt to give clear guidance to those teachers who have had little experience of 'active teaching' either from the time when they themselves were at school or during their teaching career.

It is extremely important to emphasise that numeracy is a much broader and more complex term than competence in arithmetic. It certainly should not be thought of as a 'back to basics' approach. Developing children's numeracy includes expecting children to perform many calculations mentally using strategies like doubling and halving, rounding up and down. It requires a greater emphasis on number lines and grids and less on counting sets of objects to find totals. A wide ranging discussion on numeracy can be found in *Teaching Numeracy*, Merttens (1997).

Adjusting to a numeracy programme that dictates teaching styles will be quite a challenge for some individual teachers. It is unlikely that the next National Curriculum will leave teaching styles entirely at the discretion of teachers.

The importance of a whole school picture

The coordinator needs to know how much time is spent in the teaching and learning of mathematics *throughout* the school. This may sound an inconsequential task but it isn't. Having looked at teachers' timetables in a number of different schools it is not at all easy to determine when mathematics happens, for how long, and whether this is for *all* children — including those with special educational needs. Difficulty in determining the time spent on mathematics can arise because:

- the ways in which teachers present curriculum information on their timetables may vary between Key Stage 1 and Key Stage 2. The style of timetable layout used by teachers in the two key stages may be very different; to accommodate, for example, a more topic-based approach at Key Stage 1;
- break times, lunch times, and the length of the school day may vary between different classes. So, just counting maths sessions won't give an accurate total of the amount of time spent on mathematics. You need to know how long the sessions are in each class to do the necessary calculation and to gain a perspective of the range of experiences available to children;
- some children with SEN are withdrawn from lessons, others may be withdrawn for language support or for an able-children's group. (If they are withdrawn from mathematics lessons, you need to know how their entitlement to a full mathematics curriculum is being preserved.)

Anomalies do appear and some are perfectly justifiable. Parents, for example, may ask questions about the time spent teaching maths. They may ask why their children now appear to be 'doing less/more maths' than they did when they first came to the school. Is it true? Can it be explained? Can it be justified? In many cases an apparent anomaly doesn't exist.

It's difficult to justify a difference of half an hour or more per week between, say, two parallel Year 5 classes. In the course of an inspection, inspectors will look closely at how much maths time is available to the children. Do you know? The information could be gathered for all subjects at the same time at a staff meeting when everyone brings their personal class timetable. If you've already had an inspection then the calculation may well have been done because inspectors need to know whether the school meets the recommended weekly hours total for the curriculum and this is sometimes totalled from the time given to each subject.

You could ask colleagues to do an hours sheet for maths. At a meeting you could then discuss any variations. Where it becomes clear that teachers work in different ways, there are important issues to be explored. Some teachers may be teaching most of their mathematics through topics while others tackle it mainly as a separate subject. It's fine to have this variety but if there is variation in the amount of time spent on mathematics then someone will ask you whether there is an issue of equality of opportunity to be considered.

Headteachers have been faced with a dramatic increase in administrative work. This has limited their opportunities to maintain a detailed overview of the curriculum. As a consequence the coordinator is the only person likely to have an overview of the subject curriculum. It's an example of the increasing pressure coming from an expanding expectation of the coordinator's role which is not always balanced by an improved inward flow of information to the individual concerned. And of course, there is more to be known than can be known by one person.

During the week of an inspection, teachers are asked to produce a timetable for each day. Timetables that look very different may give the impression of a lack of unity and consistency. Two Year 1 teachers working in adjacent classes may plan and work closely together — both excellent teachers. On a timetable, or in their short-term planning, one teacher may write *topic*, meaning maths, while the other may write *topic*, meaning many things but *never* maths. Trying to determine the quantity of children's mathematical experience from this kind of information is difficult. What is perhaps of more concern to the coordinator is the impression of disunity that idiosyncratic timetables and short-term planning sheets may convey to outsiders. As ever, it's a matter of finding a comfortable balance. Elsewhere in this chapter, I argue *against* the adoption of a standardised and uniform *short-term* planning sheet for all teachers.

The following chart (Figure 3.1) provides a way of collecting qualitative as well as quantitative information about maths provision across the school. It could be introduced to colleagues at a meeting, and quickly modified to make it appropriate to your school and colleagues could take a copy away to fill in. The completed forms could then be circulated and discussed at a future meeting.

Working with the structure of the National Curriculum

The last curriculum revision has not reduced the enormous number of learning objectives to an easily manageable amount. The learning objectives are not all in a logical or hierarchical sequence. This means that many teachers cannot easily see the curriculum in a developmental way. It is difficult to plan a route for a class or a small group of pupils through some parts of it. There are still many gaps within each programme of study and this makes it difficult to plan for the teaching of measures, for example. The level of detail varies enormously between one learning objective and another and this makes it difficult to plan a teaching programme. One learning objective may take weeks to work on, whilst another is swiftly dealt with. This is why some schools rely heavily on a published scheme, arguing that the scheme provides the guidance about coverage. Unfortunately this is not always true. Many schemes overdo the practice of written number computation and do not encourage oral work. Few schemes provide access to *using and applying*. Many chop up the measures pages and scatter them through the pages of textbooks and workbooks so that there is no effective development of skills.

Teachers can easily feel overwhelmed when trying to turn the learning objectives into a coherent and valuable set of experiences for children. A coordinator will inevitably face

How much time is spent on maths activity?	Class 1	Class 2	Class 3 ...
Teacher directed *practical lessons* with the whole class: mainly involving children working with equipment, resources including IT and working under close direction.			
Exposition to the whole class: mainly teacher-led explanation, showing, telling, explaining and questioning, inviting lengthy public explanations from individual children.			
Collaborative group work: mainly small groups of children discussing ideas, solving practical problems, working on investigations together with guidance but without being teacher led.			
Individual work: mainly consolidation or practise by tackling word problems and exercises from textbooks and worksheets with minimal discussion between pupils other than requests for help when unsure what to do.			
Cross-curriculum work: individual children and small groups using maths to support study in another curriculum area, e.g. measures work and data handling originating from history, science, or geography			
Individuals or small groups withdrawn from class: (SEN, able pupil programmes, language support...)			
Individuals working with learning support staff or parent volunteer...			

FIG 3.1
Collecting information on maths provision in the school

the task of planning ways to reorganise and modify the official documents to make them useful for planning and teaching the curriculum. This is now a major part of the coordinator's work.

Managing to cover the learning objectives and to offer children quality experiences will remain a major problem for teachers for some time to come. An effective way for coordinators to support colleagues is to ensure the development of high quality *medium-term* planning (which in some ways is synonymous with a scheme of work). In many schools the medium-term planning covers two, three or four years, with each year divided into; two week, half term or termly blocks — depending on the traditional work pattern within the school. The most effective medium-term plans are then easily read in time units that the teacher feels comfortable about managing. The learning objectives identified in each planning block need to be achievable in the time given. At present, we are all learning about how to get this right. Modifications are inevitable in the light of experience. Teachers in Year 2 and Year 6 have special problems because SATs are introduced at the beginning of the summer term, so these classes have much less than a year in which to cover new work. It follows that in both key stages, the *order* in which topics are covered is crucial: you can't leave important aspects of the number work until the summer term in Year 2 or Year 6! Some schools are using most of Year 2 and Year 6 to revise — a consequence of what is in effect a public examination at the end of each Key Stage.

Coordinators need to address a number of difficulties that teachers face when working within the structure of the National Curriculum if they are to be able to support their colleagues. Teachers' difficulties include:
- managing the large number of learning objectives, many containing complex ideas packed into terse phrases (learning how to 'unpack' the learning objectives, in today's jargon);
- the absence of explicit links between learning objectives that draw on similar skills and knowledge; both within each Programme of Study and between different

Programmes of Study. For example, a lack of linkage between, *number and algebra* and *shape, space and measures*, where similar skills and ideas are divorced by a knowledge structure which follows classical lines at the expense of what we know about learning;

■ the lack of guidance about ways in which links can be made between learning objectives in *using and applying* and those in the content areas of the curriculum; (made more difficult by lack of government commitment to the Non-Statutory Guidance which provides excellent support but which has not been revised since 1991);

■ depending too closely on a published scheme that purports to provide solutions — especially where *using and applying* is concerned.

Mathematical literacy and *using and applying* mathematics

The *using and applying* Programme of Study statements are crucial to the understanding of mathematics. Although presented in National Curriculum documents as learning objectives, they can be viewed differently. It can be very helpful to see the statements in terms of the *teaching styles* that are needed in order to provide children with the appropriate learning opportunities. It is useful to ask, 'What do we need to do in our teaching that allows children to demonstrate understanding of the different statements or learning objectives?'

One of the vital roles we have is to teach *mathematical literacy* and I want to deal with this first. Then we need to look at how the teaching of mathematical literacy relates to *using and applying*, both when viewed as learning objectives and as a guide to the necessary teaching styles.

The central role of literacy

The phrase 'the language of mathematics' is a frequently used one. It often refers to the learning of object names, e.g. triangle, square, pyramid, graph, table chart; and to the names of operations like, addition, subtraction, take away and so on. It is vitally important to extend the meaning of mathematical language beyond this and recognise that children need to be *mathematically literate*. The Programme of Study statements for *using and applying* provide important guidance on how to develop children's mathematical literacy. However, the key factor in promoting mathematical literacy is the teacher's classroom performance.

The opportunity for children to discuss ideas and express their own opinions is crucial. Discussion should not be seen just in terms of answering the teacher's carefully posed questions. Posing good questions is an essential part of the process but it is not enough on its own. David Pimm's book *Speaking Mathematically* (1987) discusses many of the ideas raised here. In discussing mathematical literacy, Ruth Merttens (1997) uses the phrase 'reading the mathematics' and she gives the verb 'to read' a very rich, eclectic feel. She argues that for children to be mathematically literate, they need to have a diverse range of approaches to 'reading'. When they can make a thick, rather than a thin interpretation, their reading of the mathematics informs them about what to *do* next, what to *think about* and what *techniques* to use. If they can make a thick, multi-layered reading and thereby recognise a range of meanings, they become increasingly aware of possibilities and possible interpretations. In contrast, a thin reading leaves children with perhaps only one interpretation and few strategies for checking whether they're right. A thin reading can easily leave them unable to perform *even when they already have all the knowledge and the skills necessary for the task.*

Whether one makes a thick, interpretative reading, or a thin literal one depends not only on 'reading ability' but also on the social setting and the climate of the classroom. Socially speaking, the making of thick, interpretative readings demands self expression, stating an opinion, having a viewpoint, potential disagreement, not doing what the textbook (or the teacher) might have expected. There are some classrooms where it does not pay to make thick interpretative readings of what to do when you tackle mathematics. Children's mathematical literacy is limited in classrooms where interpretations are not welcome, and where children have few opportunities for expressing opinion. It is also limited in classrooms where any opinion is acceptable and where ideas are not challenged and tested. Children's mathematical literacy cannot develop in socially oppressive, or laissez faire, classrooms. Thus an important part of the work of the coordinator is to help teachers explore their teaching styles. Children need to be taught and guided if they are to become effective readers of mathematics. For this to happen, some teachers are going to have to change their styles dramatically. Substantially more time has to be given over to children's talk about maths than has generally been allowed in maths lessons in Britain.

Krutetskii (1972) provides an interesting account of an unusual teacher whom he met in a Moscow school. Her children's examination results for mathematics were unusually and consistently high, though the pupils followed exactly the same rather formal and rigid curriculum as every other school in the district. Krutetskii observed some lessons and discovered that the teacher spent a good part of many mathematics lessons, getting individual children to read problems out loud. The class then spent a long time debating the possible meanings. They looked at the different ways in which the words and phrases could be accentuated. They discussed the different meanings that could be given to the problems. These discussions were prolonged by the teacher rather than cut short. When the problems had been interpreted, the children set to work on the mathematics. Krutetskii found that the children had considerably more understanding about what was being asked of them, mathematically. They were better able to associate what they already knew with what was required. Not only did the teaching cover mathematical knowledge, skills, techniques and general strategies, the pupils were being helped towards a greater mathematical literacy and the result was an improvement in their performance.

Mathematical statements are dense and general. Sums like 47–29 don't refer to anything in particular. Mathematically, this is a strength. Pedagogically, it is a problem, particularly for children who need to think things through by considering a specific context. Teachers can help children by getting them to read a sum like 47–29 in many different ways. Children can invent different contexts and try different strategies. Subtraction can be seen as the difference between two points on the number line. Finding the difference between two numbers on a number line is often most easily done by counting on. We adults may well read 47–29 in such a way that the possibility occurs to us to count on. We may see the 29 as being only 1 away from 30, for example. Children who are poor readers of mathematical situations will often avoid looking for a flexible approach. And so may very able children.

The context has a powerful effect on children's decision making. When asked by his mother, who is herself a professor of mathematics education, 'Matthew can you do forty-seven take away twenty-nine?' Matthew immediately began to mentally compute the answer. He was silent for longer than his mother expected. When she asked what he was doing, he began to describe a decomposition method. When she showed her surprise and asked why he hadn't counted on, Matthew replied in frustration, 'But you said take away!'

For Matthew and for many children in school, the requirement to 'do' some mathematics is bound up in a context where the 'doing' is at the behest of someone else. Rather than reading subtraction as a counting-on process the teacher's message is carefully interpreted to see what other clues are being given. In Matthew's case the clue was, 'take away.'

Poor readers often have just one strategy (or none). Good readers are more secure, more adaptable, more likely to choose alternative strategies. 'It says subtract but I'm going to count on because 29 is only 1 away from 30 and 30 up to 47 is easy.' For mathematically fluent readers, the mathematics speaks to them and they can speak to it and about it.

There are plenty of opportunities to develop mathematical literacy through extended discussion. For example:
- at the beginning of a topic, when vocabulary, skills and techniques are being introduced;

- at the beginning of a topic, when it is important that children make strong cognitive links with what they have already learned;
- when a problem solving activity or a mathematical investigation demands that children *interpret* a task and discuss the range of possible meanings;
- at the beginnings and ends of individual lessons, when children can practise incorporating new words and phrases into their descriptions of what they have learned and achieved;
- during lessons, when ideas are being established and challenged and where children are finding the reading of certain bits of mathematics difficult;
- at the end of a lesson, when the teacher can encourage a drawing together of ideas, a comparison of results, or an interpretation of findings;
- at the end of a topic, when children can give a presentation to the class about their discoveries.

Using and applying in relation to teaching styles

It's important for the teacher to create situations where children can *demonstrate* acquisition of the *using and applying* learning objectives. We need to bring children's knowledge and skills out into the open. Not only do children then have greater opportunity to acquire knowledge and skills from each other, but we get a clear feel for what different children can do. This information is the heart of assessment. It is generated very effectively when children are actively solving mathematical problems that require them to make decisions both individually and together in small collaborative groups.

Teachers are helped to form judgments of children's abilities when the children publicly demonstrate their knowledge, skills and techniques. The richest opportunities come when the children are given opportunities to **show that they know what to do when they *don't* know what to do**. They need opportunities to demonstrate that they can get themselves unstuck by calling up the necessary knowledge, skills, techniques and general strategies, by themselves wherever possible. Changing the teaching style changes the emphasis.

Let's take an example. Suppose I want children to explore some algebraic ideas about using a mathematical rule to generate a series of numbers. The *way* that I choose to present an investigation plays a part in determining which learning objectives they can demonstrate. So, my teaching style influences which aspects of *using and applying* the children can practice, develop and demonstrate. The first teaching style gives the rule and thereby prevents the children discovering it.

I organise them into small groups and give each group a card on which is written:

Here are two rules to follow:
1   If you have an even number you must halve it to find the next number in the sequence.
2   If you have an odd number, you must multiply it by 3 and add 1 to find the next number in the sequence.

I tell them to choose any number, try to decide which rule will apply and to see what happens as they work. They must tell each other their ideas and can't go on until they all agree and can say why they agree.

Children's response
A small group of two or three children working together have to explain their reasoning. This is a hard entry point to the problem requiring high levels of literacy and ability to collaborate. They have to listen, compare ideas and argue before moving on. They are likely to tackle only a few numbers especially if they are part of a group that enjoy lengthy discussion. What they won't be able to do in this instance is to work out what the rule is. It's been stated at the outset. If I want to give them an opportunity to *discover the rule*, I need to present the starting point in a different way.

Providing an opportunity to discover rules
I give everyone in a small group a card each, on which I've written the following numbers:

After Eight	I begin to read it out.
56, 28, 14, 7, 22,	'56, 28, 14, 7,(and so on). Oh! That's strange.'
11, 34,	'Oh! how funny.'
17, 52,	'What's going on?'
26, 13, 40,	'That's weird.'
20, 10, 5, 16,	'Something funny again.'
8	'Eight! What happens after eight, I wonder? What's the next number going to be?'

I introduce this to a small group sitting together. We start a discussion about what might be happening. I tell them to try things out on their own for ten minutes before joining forces as a group. They will need to explain to each other what they've done individually. Later, I will press them to describe in their own words what they've found out. Then they will have to write the problem down on a poster along with their findings. My experience is that most children find the halving rule first. I've hinted but not said that two rules are involved. Conceptually, handling two rules at the same time is much harder than handling either of them separately.

Through my opening commentary I try to stress those places where the rules change and I vary the amount of support at this point so that the children have just enough information to get started but don't have everything spelled out. I want them to have plenty of opportunity to reason, to spot that two rules are operating and to suggest what the rules are. They have an opportunity to deduce the rules from the evidence available. They also have an opportunity to decide how to work, (calculator or not, table square or not) and how to present their findings on the poster.

Review

This is a hard entry point and requires good literacy and collaborative skills. The task is structured but with little intended intervention if all goes according to plan. Mathematical literacy is being tested in this activity because the children have to deduce what to *do*. What thoughts and actions are needed? What pictures need to be created in their minds and on their posters as a result of *reading the mathematics* in the broadest sense?

Being literate in this activity means being able to *read* all the possible meanings contained within the sequence. It means:

- *interpreting* the signs as objects which have meaning;
- realising that the value of each symbol determines the value of the next;
- understanding that the string of symbols has an internal structure that is determined by application of the (initially) unknown rules.

Literacy means being able to deduce how to carry out actions on each of the symbols, how to take into account the way in which elements interact with each other, how to *assemble meaning* from the symbols themselves and from what is produced when they have been acted on. A challenging and timely discussion which explores many issues relating to narrative and reality, can be found in Bruner (1996, pp. 130–49).

An easier entry point

I sit a group on the carpet or on chairs around a flip chart and scribe for the children as we talk.

'Who can tell me how to recognise an odd number? ... What about even numbers?'
'I want you to look at the numbers I write down.'
'Karen, I've got a job for you. Every time you see me write an *odd* number, I'd like you to help me by working out three times that number. Then we'll add 1 to the number you tell me and I'll write it down. Let's do a couple for practice ... If I say 5, you check to see if it's odd. If it *is*, then we'll multiply it by 3 and then we'll add 1. 16? Are you sure?'

'Assim, when I write an *even* number I want you to help me by halving the number for me. If you get stuck you can choose someone to help you. And when we've done few together we'll talk about what we notice. Then you can all choose some numbers to try out on your own.'

Commentary

The advantage here is that the arithmetic is being done for most children in the group, though they will be asked to calculate mentally, check Karen's and Assim's answers, and spot errors. They are being asked to decide each time whether a number is odd or even and to say which of the two children has to do the next calculation. So the rule is left pretty well unstated. The work that most of them have to do is to *associate* a number with either Karen or Assim. The task for most children, then, is to *interpret* the number that has just been generated. I'm scribing, so I'm reducing the need for children to pay attention to recording. In this way, hopefully, I'm freeing their attention for specific bits of maths that I've chosen to focus on. I'll ask each time who they think has to do the next calculation: 'Is this one for Assim to do or for Karen . . . Why?'

For those children lacking confidence or expertise, this is a lesson in watching and listening to others as they work. I will ask less able or less knowledgeable members of the group if they agree with what's been said or if they would like to choose a starting number. Because some sequences are very long and can also produce large numbers, I might choose half a dozen beforehand, write them on blank playing cards and ask certain people in the group to take a card. I will involve the least able by asking them what they think is going on. I need to know what they find difficult so I can help them find a more independent way of working in future — though in this session some may do no more than watch and listen. The other children and I are providing them with a *model* of how to work in this type of lesson.

Teachers need to lead and manage some of the discussion process. Some discussion needs to be with the whole class. Just as important, there should be a chance for pairs and small groups to work without the direct intervention of the teacher, and for the teacher to work with a small group for an extended period of time without interruption. The subject leader has a crucial role to play in helping colleagues become successful in the use of these complex teaching styles.

Getting the most out of using and applying

Teachers need to know the extent of their children's mathematical literacy, and children need opportunities to show teachers how well they are performing. *Using and applying* provides a useful framework. Things to do:

- include references to *using and applying* statements when planning maths activities from, *number and algebra, shape space and measures, handling data*;
- re-write the *using and applying* statements as 'I can do' phrases and use them to let the children know what you expect them to do during the lesson;
- give the children copies of relevant 'I can do' statements and let them fill these in themselves;
- *actively teach* and demonstrate how to use and apply mathematics in practical tasks;
- provide opportunities for *discussion* to help children improve the way they select and use mathematics that is appropriate to the task;
- *actively teach* children to *ask* (as well as answer) questions including, 'What would happen if . . .'.

It's hard for the subject leader to help colleagues develop in the ways suggested unless there is time to work alongside them in classrooms. When you do have these opportunities you have real examples to take as discussion points. By focusing on what teachers actually do in lessons, there is much more chance of creating situations where children are performing effectively.

One way is to focus on what you want the children to do:
- 'develop different mathematical approaches and look for ways to overcome difficulties,'
- 'discuss their work, respond to and ask mathematical questions' . . .

With the subject leader and a colleague working together in the same classroom, the teacher's chosen style and the children's responses can be observed and discussed. Through planning, observation and subsequent discussion it is possible for the subject leader to help colleagues make links between teaching strategies and the children's subsequent behaviour. Teachers are then in a much stronger position to encourage those aspects of children's behaviour that they wish to strengthen.

Coordinators may well have to accept that their teaching style becomes a model for adoption by other teachers for a while — and this can feel uncomfortable — particularly for a young teacher, recently promoted and working with colleagues with many more years' classroom experience.

My argument then is that if development of effective learning within *using and applying* becomes something that a coordinator tackles in their school with colleagues (and it has to be tackled together if it is to be a whole school development), then it has to be tackled at the level of teaching behaviour. Responding to requests for activities for children 'to help with *using and applying*' is unlikely to improve matters sufficiently in the long-term and may only serve to obscure the main issues.

Chapter 4   The National Curriculum content areas

Number and numeracy

Number and numeracy have become central in the public debate about mathematics. Children's performance in number has been the subject of several recent publications, including the TIMSS report, Harris, (1997). The evidence from the test results obtained so far, suggests a decline in children's performance in arithmetic compared to children from other countries. Concern has also been voiced because many teachers express greater confidence about teaching number than about other areas of the mathematics curriculum.

The quality of current debate

The coordinator has to deal with enquiries from parents, the press and other outside agencies. There are parents' meetings to manage and all parents will have been influenced in some way by the education debate. It's difficult to keep both an open and a receptive mind when helping parents and others interpret reports on national and local standards in mathematics. The accuracy and meaning of the information gained from recent reports is not easy to judge.

The debates that the subject manager has to conduct on behalf of the school are not made easier by the behaviour of government ministers and spokespeople. Both the last and the current government have become embroiled in showing that they 'care about education'. Despite the fact that many politicians genuinely care, the nature of public political debate is such that there are severe limitations on what views they can express. Demonstrating a high level of care requires short sound-bites and loud public condemnation of teachers when there is any suggestion of standards going into decline, while the response to news of improving standards is equally constrained but in a different way. News of improvements in GCSE or A-level results requires mute congratulation and heavy scepticism.

It will take a while for politicians to re-position themselves in relation to constructive debates about education. In the meantime, what is regularly overlooked is that OFSTED reports for most primary schools show a large majority of lessons as satisfactory or better. What teachers are actually doing is trying to raise standards from a relatively high base, not from a low one. The suggestion that there is a disaster about to happen is unhelpful scaremongering. We are in the middle of a political campaign to raise standards in schools where the opportunity for informed and impartial debate has yet to be established securely.

Developments to the number curriculum

The evidence suggests that there are undoubtedly considerable improvements still to be made in the teaching of mathematics and in children's performance. Some of the improvements are relatively easy to put in place and could have a significant effect on standards. Many changes do not require financing but some most certainly do. The changes encouraged and discussed in this book include:

- the active teaching of maths as a practical subject for a considerable proportion of the time;
- developing opportunities for children to discuss mathematical ideas;
- ensuring that children get no less than an hour each day of mathematically related activity;
- releasing well qualified subject leaders from their own class teaching responsibilities on a regular basis to work with colleagues.

Developing the number curriculum is now most urgent and demands close attention. The quickest way to improve standards is to focus sympathetically and creatively on raising the quality of teaching. We need to establish a common agreement on what it means to be numerate and what we expect children to be able to do in the name of numeracy. What do we mean when we say we want children to have a 'feel for number'? This debate needs to be carried out in school between colleagues to establish the range and diversity of views held.

There is a need to develop children's mental facility considerably further than has been done of late. This may require having lessons devoted to numeracy throughout the full range of both key stages. Being numerate includes the ability to:

- describe and discuss, as well as to demonstrate, an awareness of numerical processes;
- an ability to internalise mental pictures of number lines and number squares;
- an ability to recall number bonds, complements to ten, and addition and multiplication facts;
- an awareness of the relationships between different arithmetic processes;
- the ability to estimate and approximate, to round up and down to the next ten and to use doubling and halving.

In particular, there is a need to increase the time spent on improving and developing children's mental computation skills. The target is that most children should be able to perform most of the calculations associated with their age or ability group as **mental calculations without pencil and paper**, and to demonstrate flexibility in their choice of ways of tackling mental problems. Two useful books of activities and ideas for number work at Key Stages 1 and 2 are published by BEAM (BE A Mathematician). The books cover:

- working in different ways;
- the importance of discussion;
- teaching and assessing.

The children's activity pages provide work in the key areas of: mental maths, number lines and grids, calculators, working with apparatus and pencil and paper.

The advantages of numeracy lessons

A typical example in a Key Stage 1 class involved the children in tabletop maths games every Wednesday. The teacher provided a range of board and other games. Some games involved combining throws of two or more dice. Children played the games of their choice with a partner and all moves were calculated mentally with the aid of fingers and a large number line on the wall where necessary. The lessons always ended with a ten minute teacher-led discussion of interesting games and fascinating scores. The children had to retell some of the more interesting scores and describe how they had calculated them. The teacher then invited other children to carry out the same calculation in another way. The teacher drew children's attention to particularly efficient and easy strategies, like rounding up to the nearest decade, counting on in twos or fives, and doubling and halving.

Although many schools provide plenty of practical activity there are still many others where this is not current practice. Few schools have established policies where very young children are asked to talk in carefully directed sessions about the processes of mental calculation that they use to solve number problems. The fact that some nursery schools and classes have established this type of work is a clear signal that it is possible with older children.

The amount of content in the number curriculum creates pressure for coverage at the expense of understanding. The current numeracy debate is unashamedly about understanding. There is a tendency for teachers to rush children far too soon into written computation and undirected calculator work. If children are to acquire sound mental computation strategies, then it will take time to establish teaching routines throughout the school. As a whole school policy for daily mental practise is established, people may assume that for a while, children may not cover as much of the number curriculum as before. This is by no means certain.

In one junior school, on the northern edge of Birmingham, teachers conduct a numeracy session at the start of every mathematics lesson throughout the school, every day. It takes twenty minutes a day and has been established for a few years. It has not forced a narrowing of the mathematics curriculum. The school provides rich and diverse opportunities across all areas of the subject. The children's performance in number is above average especially in mental mathematics. Whatever happened when the school introduced the scheme, these pupils are now ahead of most children of similar age. In their mental work and in number work generally, they know more, about more.

Preparing for the future

Coordinators need to be making plans for increasing the time spent on developing children's numeracy skills. If a 'numeracy hour' is imposed by government you need to be prepared. It is important to feel very comfortable with the plans you make if you are to help colleagues to make changes to deep rooted practice. The more confident you are that you have got it right for your children, the more likely you are to help colleagues make creative developments to their teaching. Your confidence will help others to creatively mediate the changes that are still to come.

Separate numeracy lessons provide opportunities to focus on *skills* and *techniques* (like doubling and halving), whilst lessons about measures and lessons that have a cross-curriculum link with science, geography, design and technology, etc. are ideal for developing practical work, practising skills and techniques and are really useful for helping children to develop *strategies* (i.e. knowing which skills and techniques to use in a situation). By providing both types of lessons during the same period of time (a week or fortnight for older children; a day or two for reception children), teachers can provide some specific lessons that focus on developing numeracy and others that develop the ability to apply number skills to practical situations involving measures.

Algebra

Algebra can be an exciting and pleasurable activity for children at Key Stage 1. Many adults associate the word only with work they experienced at secondary school, but much can be done in the early years that is interesting and has strong links with *using and applying*.

The use of practical activities related to pattern work in other curriculum areas provides starting points for mathematical investigations and recording. Colleagues will want to know, *what* to emphasise and *how* to develop ideas in mathematics lessons about simple algebraic relationships which have emerged from starting points elsewhere in the curriculum. Children do not soak up the maths inherent in PE, art or music: the teacher needs to **make the mathematics explicit** by taking topics in one subject and providing time in maths lessons to explore them further; by discussion of pattern, prediction of what comes next, inventing and using symbols to communicate ideas and to plan further work. What makes the work explicitly mathematical is discussion and prediction about **what will come next** based on an analysis of the pattern that is already known.

One way of thinking about algebra is to regard it as a set of rules or instructions. The rules that govern the placing of the next bead on the string are rules of procedure — algebraic rules. The rules of procedure for a sequence of three movements in PE or the production of three sounds in music give the algebra of the situation. By getting young children to perform practical tasks in different areas of the curriculum and then looking at ways of predicting what will come next in a given situation, and later, by representing the sequences through pictures, invented signs and symbols, teachers can get children to work with the algebra of each situation. By understanding the algebra, children know how to perform when asked to make sounds given the rules: loud, soft, soft soft, loud, soft soft, soft . . . They can use their understanding of the algebra to invent and use symbols to plan the performance and they can read the symbols later on to reproduce the music. Aileen Duncan's (1992) book for primary teachers on teaching algebra is a useful source.

Coordinators can encourage colleagues to work from their own strengths in PE, music, and art. PE offers children kinaesthetic experiences of mathematics. They can plan and produce a sequence of moves, e.g. a move from high to low position ending in a balance using three body parts, followed by a roll and a jump to standing. Children can devise signs and symbols to represent moves and can then work on these in the classroom. The symbols can be used to plan further work in PE either as an individual or in groups so that two or three children can present a combined performance. The teacher can draw attention to the mathematics by giving time in mathematics lessons to the preparation of the symbols and the discussion. Teachers can emphasise that this is maths by drawing attention to the fact that it is about **inventing and using symbols** to represent movement and position, planning sequences and looking at repeating patterns (of body movements). Many teachers are encouraging children to work in a similar way when working on the composing strand of the music curriculum. Teachers have encouraged children to produce repeating patterns in art. There is an opportunity to draw children's attention to the fact that the work can be mathematical, if the children discuss the patterns and their arrangements and make some predictions about what comes next, in the patterns they are devising in different curriculum areas.

Hughes's (1984) work with 3 and 4 year olds is interesting in this context. Intriguingly, in the school situation, some children including those with special needs can solve the calculations involved in these hidden cube problems more accurately and efficiently than when they have to calculate with the cubes in view.

When children can predict what comes next, they are working algebraically. Work can involve threading cubes to continue the pattern Yellow, Red, Yellow, Red, Yellow, ... making hand or potato prints, using coins or stamps, etc. Hiding games provide another useful activity where children count some cubes (say 8) and watch while they are covered with a cloth. One child is invited to put their hand under the cloth and take some but not all of the cubes. They pull the cubes out into the open and count them. The teacher simply asks the group to say how many remain hidden. No instructions about counting on or back but children are invited to think the numbers in their head or use their fingers if they want. The teacher observes the chosen strategies and encourages discussion. The children are working algebraically when they recognise the rules that need to be applied to the situation. Most may choose to use counting on but some may count back, others will change subsets to something more manageable. For example, by saying: Eight under the cloth. Three taken out. Four and four make eight. Here's three so there must be five. On being questioned their ability to explain their thinking will improve. The teacher is signalling acceptance of an important basic rule that many anxious children don't follow — viz. it's OK to change the given calculation into something equivalent that is easier to manage. The Open University (1991) published a useful set of books for teachers which includes one on the nature of Algebra as part of its PM649 course 'Supporting Primary Mathematics'.

At the upper end of Key Stage 1 and at Key Stage 2 we are looking to extend children's experiences of pattern into more abstract areas. The Open University video (1991) is useful because it shows coordinators working in different situations including a lesson on algebra based on pattern making using Cuisenaire rods. The coordinator helps the children develop the necessary vocabulary to extend their ability to describe and predict more abstract patterns. Observing other coordinators at work can serve as a useful role model.

Shape, space and measures

The National Curriculum demands very uneven levels of understanding across work within each Key Stage. Levels 1 and 2 demand little more than basic recognition and naming. Not much is demanded in terms of mathematical *ability or application.*

Many children arrive at school with plenty of informal knowledge of 2D and 3D shapes — not just in the experiential sense that is inevitable from growing up in the world but literally knowing many of the ideas that are assessed at level 1. Many can already work with 3D and 2D shapes, use everyday language to describe properties and positions, and can measure and order objects using direct comparison. What the coordinator can do is find ways to move this demand for memorisation into some useful mathematical activity that demands suitable mathematical challenges for children.

What's missing from the National Curriculum is a demand to practise sliding back and forth between the ideas and skills associated with 2D and 3D shape. Helen Williams, a consultant and a reception teacher of many years standing has developed several activities that help develop this greater fluidity of thinking.

Helen suggests the use of 3D models of cubes and prisms made from Clixi or Polydron together with 2D drawings of nets. Children lay the Clixi on the net and build up to a 3D model and then break it down (perhaps when practised) to a different net. By asking children to make 'pictures in your head', ask them to make a cube from dough or 'Blutack' and to imagine it cut through in different ways. Spend a few seconds imagining what the new faces will look like before cutting with a knife. Can they guess what different 2D nets will build into? Can they draw their own pictures of what they think each will become? Can they slice a cube of Blutack and create different 2D faces? With a single cut each time, is it possible to make a square with one cut, an oblong or rectangle, a diamond, a triangle? Can they use six Clixi squares to build some arrangements of six that will fold to make a cube and some that won't? Can they say in advance which are which? Can they pick one and say *why* it will do what they claim?

That's well within the reach of a bright 5 year old. It's richer than level 1 requires. It's richer than what is required at level 2 (use mathematical names for common 3D and 2D shapes and describe their properties, including numbers of sides and corners). It demands more than a mechanical knowledge of content at level 1 and demands a subtle knowledge of the way the level one content can link together. It's about being a mathematician when you're aged five and the National

Curriculum can't ensure that. Sliding from one piece of content into another is the key that Helen uses to unlock children's minds. If these practical challenges are set for some children in the classroom they soon leak into other groups and the climate of the classroom changes. It becomes a place where children make links between areas of content knowledge, through the teacher's adoption of teaching styles that are chosen to force children into positions where they can't fail to display some of the behaviours listed under *using and applying*.

Children also enjoy working with elastics. I use 4m lengths of thin knicker elastic (less than 1cm wide) knotted into a loop. There's room enough inside a loop for up to five children and they need to work collaboratively to produce shapes. The faces have to be imagined as the children use their waists as vertices. Three people inside can only make triangular patterns! The use of elastics with reception children is discussed in an article in *Mathematics Teaching*, **129**, December 1989, pp. 48–49).

Instead of labelling children as level 2 or above and pushing them on to 'new and harder work' which is what a fragmented and hierarchical National Curriculum may be seen to encourage us to do with very capable 4 and 5 year olds, we need to reinforce the connections children have made between different areas of knowledge. Since many children start school with some of the level 1 skills and knowledge already fairly well glued in place, there is time to help them build some strong links *across* the maths curriculum and into other curriculum areas within levels 1 and 2 and firmly consolidate what they know before moving onto new material.

Making links between curriculum areas and teaching to ensure a depth of understanding requires a review of planning and teaching. It is something that the coordinator needs to consider carefully. If pushing children on to harder and harder maths is the only strategy used in your school, then many children and teachers will see maths simply as the acquisition of new information and skills. Conversely, they will see little value in dwelling on a mathematical topic out of interest, or sticking with an idea in order to gain understanding. A more effective approach for teachers and children alike is to move children sideways, strengthening cross links between different Programmes of Study and subject areas rather than upwards (or downwards according to your view of the National Curriculum levels). Working across the Programmes of Study also has the effect of keeping the class together on the same topic and allowing whole class teaching to remain an option for teachers, whilst at the same time allowing differentiation through a range of tasks, thus ensuring able children are challenged.

The coordinator has a key role to play in opening up this discussion and supporting colleagues who are searching for resources and techniques to extend able children in the class whilst at the same time needing activities that provide consolidation for the less able. So often, this tension, which is difficult to resolve especially with large classes, leads to fragmentation and children working individually on disparate topics. Once this has become established it is extremely hard to return to a whole class topic. Instead the teacher acts as a service engineer, providing equipment, resources and instructions about what children have to do next, but never able to teach and discuss mathematics with any of them.

The importance of measures

In primary schools, measures work is very important because it can provide a unifying role, bringing together many of the things we try to do in our teaching. It draws on ideas relating to number and calculation and creates practical situations where our numeracy skills need to be applied. We can pull together three important elements of our work: developing children's mathematical thinking; teaching useful strategies and techniques; observing and assessing children's performance in mathematical problem solving.

Tackling problems within the context of measures brings children's ability to *use* mathematics out into the open. The teaching of measures creates really useful opportunities to:
- involve children in practical tasks that pose really challenging problems;
- teach strategies like estimating in relation to distance, area, volume, mass and weight, etc. and approximation

when reading a scale to the nearest whole or half measure;

- teach techniques like: keeping an accurate count when using cupfuls, hand spans, or strides, etc.; and reading a wide range of different scales, like rulers and angle measures;
- teach children how to select and make use of appropriate mathematics;
- provide lesson time when children can discuss their own work and develop their ability to use various forms of representation;
- help children develop their ability to use mathematical language to explain, describe and use their powers of reasoning.

The latest version of the National Curriculum isn't much help to teachers when it comes to planning the teaching of measures. The documents give little guidance and advice, there is little detailed information about topics like *time* and what there is, is scattered and incoherent.

Too many young children lack opportunities for experiential learning at home with water, paint, sand, rice, etc. Many only have a limited opportunity to help with gardening, cooking or carrying out other activities involving measuring. Shopping in supermarkets offers few opportunities to observe and take part in *measuring* and most money transactions are far removed from the traditional corner-shop experience of many teachers' own childhood. Many carers are still unable to obtain quality preschool provision for the children in their care. Consequently, the nursery or reception class is still too often the first opportunity that many children get to work practically with measures and measurement in a sustained way.

Throughout the primary years a lot of the practical work in science, geography, history, and design and technology can be directly used to teach and consolidate all aspects of mathematics, particularly measures work. Where schools use topics as a basis for planning, a fortnightly period of work, for example, involving work on measures can be organised to coincide with work in science, or design and technology, etc. The teachers' planning can be designed to highlight links between the measures topic in mathematics and practical work in other subjects that demands similar knowledge and skills. The children's activities consolidate measures work in maths by creating opportunities for practical problem solving in other curriculum areas. Each teacher has the choice of whether the measures work in maths lessons will precede, run alongside, or follow the topic work in the other selected curriculum areas. Sometimes, children haven't sufficiently developed the strategies and techniques to carry out practical work in science and so the same skills can be part of a maths topic that precedes the science topic by a few days. On another occasion, the teacher might choose to introduce the strategies and skills within geography or design and technology and then consolidate them in mathematics lessons a few weeks later.

The coordinator can initiate planning for small topics based on teachers' curriculum strengths. Teachers who are strong in history and geography could be helped to teach their measures work through appropriate work in these subjects. The coordinator can then help them find appropriate consolidation activities in mathematics. When sufficient topics have been developed it will be necessary for the coordinator to take an overview that considers progression and continuity within measures work from the point of view of the mathematics curriculum.

Schools need to look at whether to include money and cost under measures or under number: there are benefits either way. Cost is something that needs to be referred to explicitly in planning documents alongside planning related to money. Ideas relating to cost appear in two distinct ways in many classrooms. In the class shop where small items or pictures of items are deliberately under-priced to keep the counting within manageable limits. Like Woolworth of old, nothing is over sixpence, but unlike the Woolworth of bygone times, the cost of items in the class shop doesn't relate to real shop prices. Some schools overcome this by buying fruit at wholesale prices and selling it to children at break time, or by the mass baking of biscuits and selling these at cost. There are real benefits to pointing out that these prices represent the real cost of half an apple, or a cheese straw. Children prefer handling real money, which, unlike the plastic variety doesn't cost the school anything (unless you lose it!).

Coordinators need to look at the range of children's experiences through the school to assess the diversity and quality of the work on offer in topics on money and cost. It is very easy to limit children's experiences to coin recognition and unnecessarily trivial and irrelevant computations whilst omitting to use real situations, for example, involving postage and receipt of letters in school, calculating the cost of trips, visits and food for parties. There are real money transactions taking place in classrooms almost everyday and real benefits to be gained by using these opportunities as part of a lesson on numeracy rather than something to rushed in order to start a lesson. These daily transactions are often under-used. If the school secretary needs the dinner money immediately then send it, but keep some cash permanently in a drawer so that the transaction can be reconstructed later with the children and some teaching points made.

The use of 10p and 1p coins for teaching place value provides a more relevant context than plastic or wooden base ten materials which are never seen outside the school context. Children's understanding of money and cost can be directly used to explore place value when this is explored regularly in terms of numbers of pounds, 10p and 1p.

Data handling

Some of the most effective work comes directly from data that has been gathered as part of a study in other curriculum areas. There are three main strands. Strand 1 is taught well, but 2 and 3 are often overlooked, see Figure 4.1 which might be used to assess development in data handling in your school.

FIG 4.1
Assessing data handling

Purpose of data handling	Where opportunities exist within the school's scheme of work
1 To collect and display data in various ways	
2 To interrogate data in the form of lists, tables, charts, graphs in order to retrieve information and report it or transform it into another format.	
3 To develop hypotheses, develop arguments and interpret information based on interrogation of data in various formats.	

The three strands of data handling

1 Collecting, organising and displaying data to provide a pictorial representation of information.
2 Information retrieval by using data collected previously as the actual source of information.
3 Interpretation and the construction of arguments and hypotheses based on the inspection of data previously organised into tables charts and graphs.

It is useful to check where these opportunities exist for teachers and children throughout the school.

When children are familiar with information technology hardware and software, its use can provide much easier access to strands 2 and 3. Tedious and distracting calculations are eliminated and data is produced in a variety of forms, allowing the children to concentrate on analysis, interpretation, and hypothesis.

❝ *Every search that children make will involve them in some analysis and interpretation — for example, identifying the ways in which data is distributed, identifying trends, or establishing*

*connections. All this will involve children in making infer-
ences and drawing conclusions. These will need to be tested
and, if necessary, the children's hypotheses will need to be
re-formulated and, perhaps, more data collected.*

(ILEA, 1988, p. 101)

Anna Lewis's book, (Lewis, 1996) contains a very useful
chapter called 'Everyday Activities', where she suggests a
wide range of things to do at different times: registration,
going out to play, lining up, tidying up, and so on. For each
situation she identifies opportunities for the teacher to ask
questions and explore ideas, and Lewis relates these to
different areas of maths that can explored in each situation,
including data handling.

Chapter 5

A broad view of mathematics

Definitions of mathematics

Different people have different views about what maths is
and what it means to learn and to teach it — and they use
different language to explain their ideas. Many people,
including a large proportion of parents, see maths as a list
of things to learn — a body of knowledge to be stored. In
contrast, many teachers talk as if mathematics is something
that is constructed in the mind — a way of thinking.
Coordinators need to communicate to many different people
about what happens in their school and it's vitally important
to be able to recognise the different viewpoints and the
language that accompanies them. It's helpful to be able to
use the language that others use and to move between the
different ideas that people express. For readers who want to
delve deeply, there is an interesting and worthwhile book
edited by Paul Ernest (1994).

One of the reasons why it can be difficult to get your point
of view across to others, is that they don't see maths the way
you do: they're literally 'talking another language'. This
explains to some extent why curriculum initiatives developed
by the coordinator and colleagues in full agreement and
following plenty of discussion and consultation can still
produce very different results in different classrooms and
can even founder despite everyone's desire for success.

We don't always mean the same things when we use words like *teaching, learning, practical work, questioning, discussion,* . . . etc. The coordinator who tries to get everyone to mean what they say and to say what they mean is unlikely to succeed. However, the coordinator who knows the range of views and theories that are held by colleagues is more easily able to manage curriculum development and can support professional development of colleagues more effectively too. It doesn't mean agreeing with everyone, or not having an opinion of your own, but it does mean developing ways of knowing what the word 'mathematics' might mean to others. Rather than take an adversarial stance, and arguing which view is right, it is more helpful to see beyond this duality. Maybe these two viewpoints are the closest we can get at the moment — so why not use them both to develop some further questions? What view of mathematics and, therefore, what value judgments are we transmitting to school children and promoting in schools? How can the two views of external knowledge and internal construction help us to develop a maths curriculum of quality for children? What can we gain by considering the two ideas together? What does it mean to put them in juxtaposition?

Which of the following statements is helpful to you? For each one, consider what story you can tell about your work as a teacher, your own classroom, your colleagues and your school? Mathematics is:

- a body of knowledge and a set of skills that can be taught and learned;
- made up of patterns and relationships which need to be learned;
- is the application of rational and logical argument to certain ideas and systems, using precise rules;
- a creative activity involving imagination, intuition and discovery;
- a way of solving problems that depends on applying general strategies to knowledge and skills;
- a means of communicating information and ideas.

(*Maths in ILEA Primary Schools: Part 1,* 1988: pp. 8–9)

Real maths and classroom maths

I've always been in a quandary about maths needing to be both classroom based and in the 'real' world. First I find I'm irritated by terminology that implies that the classroom isn't real. It was real enough for me, both as a child and as an adult! The attitudes of my two daughters express very different views and responses to maths. Hannah delighted in algebra, pattern, and what is often called pure maths. She took up Latin as soon as she could and later continued it in her own time as an extra-curriculum subject after school, partly because she saw it as mathematical and logical. She enjoyed the demands of logical and analytical thinking in maths, Latin and the puzzle books she bought from the supermarket and pored over. This maths was real enough to her, though most of it had as much immediate applicability in her life outside school as a Latin phrase book would when speaking to Italians on holiday. She chose to study philosophy at A-level partly through a continuing interest in logic. Her sister Alice would only do school maths if the teacher could explain when and how it was going to be of some use 'out there'. If the teacher's reply wasn't convincing, she didn't do it — or did it with considerable reluctance — failing to see the 'point of it'. Both views are prevalent in classrooms and are legitimate views to hold. Neither daughter chose to study maths at A-level. I'm not suggesting that school maths is simply about providing children with what pleases them. If the diet in the classroom is unvarying, it is unlikely to switch people on. A utilitarian curriculum of essential maths also represents an unacceptable narrowing of opportunities.

One important reason for going to school should be that school offers children the opportunity to explore things that they wouldn't come into contact with at home or in their community. Art, dance, sculpture, singing, and some parts of mathematics can be included in this list since they often fail to feature as participatory activities in many homes. There are aspects of mathematics which lie beyond basic number and computation and which children can find exciting. Through successful study of a broad maths curriculum, children can develop powers of logical and intuitive thinking and systematic ways of working. It has to be said though that the way in which maths is often presented leaves children feeling alienated, unsuccessful and unenthusiastic.

Many of the non-utilitarian explorations of maths are unlikely to occur by chance outside a school environment and should also be included in a broad curriculum. A mathematics curriculum of quality can broaden the mind — if it is taught well.

Qualifications in maths act as gate-keepers both in secondary school, further education and in employment. We may want to tackle the political use of examinations as barriers to future opportunities for unsuccessful candidates but we are duty bound to give children the best opportunity possible to acquire the necessary knowledge, understanding and skills to achieve examination success. This should not be seen to imply 'teaching to the test'.

The Non-Statutory Guidance remains a valuable source of advice. It is part of the National Curriculum, and a valuable part. It gives clear advice about the range and balance of work that children need. The HMI series, *Matters for Discussion*, (HMSO, 1985), although published some time ago, also gives a very clear and well organised picture of appropriate experiences for children.

Developing the curriculum in primary school

This is a complex issue and currently receives considerable attention both from within education circles and from political groups outside schools. Put very bluntly there seem to be three possibilities for teachers:

1 A knee jerk reaction to criticism and stress — give up thinking and teach only what you have been directed to teach.

2 A survival strategy and a reaction to too many changes in too short a time — continue to teach what has been taught over the years, making minimum modifications to meet legislative requirements.

3 A calm professionalism emerging from a supportive environment — review professional and philosophical

positions and teach what is judged as appropriate based on informed professional wisdom, taking into account the needs of individual children, parents, employers, other groups and the broader needs of society.

It is salutary to remind ourselves that there is no common agreement within our society on the purpose of schooling. There are deep divisions within society and this is one reason why such contradictory demands are made on teachers, schools and the education system. The parental nature of schools and schooling elicits requests for parenting from society at large. Sometimes the 'nurturing parent' is sought, sometimes the authoritarian.

Some of those who claim to speak for employers demand nothing more of children than computational skills in arithmetic — and many of those who hold this view are scathing about the use of electronic aids. However, teachers are also expected to produce children who can 'fulfil their potential', children who have broad interests and who will be able to function effectively in the world of tomorrow: a world undeniably dominated by information technology which will set the ground rules for both work and leisure. In mathematics, children need much more than a diet of pencil and paper computation practise if they are to have some quality of life as an adult.

One argument amongst social economists is that the world of full employment was a temporary phenomenon, confined to the democratic countries of western Europe during the war period of the 1940s and briefly afterwards. Before and since, and indeed outside Europe, full employment has not been a significant social feature. If so, this poses extraordinary difficulties in schools. It can be argued then that in today's primary classroom a minority of children will go on to work as adults in situations that will be highly sophisticated, challenging and financially rewarding. Their jobs will be wide ranging in type but will last for fairly brief periods after which they may train and move to jobs which have never previously existed. When they reach adulthood, this small group of children will be employed for a large proportion of their life in a highly complex post-industrial society where information technology will dominate working practice. Evidence suggests that 'intelligence' will not necessarily be a determining factor but opportunity, particularly birth and the social conditions of early childhood.

In the same classroom, today's teacher needs to help a majority of children prepare for an adult life where they may spend large periods of time unemployed or with brief periods of poorly paid work. For some, mathematics and its applications will be an important tool in their life. For everyone, an interest and enjoyment in mathematics for its own sake could help contribute to their quality of life: both those who will lead busy lives with little leisure time, as well as those whose adult lives will offer little opportunity for paid employment or relatively expensive leisure pursuits.

What sort of mathematics curriculum can teachers responsibly provide *now* to meet the needs of children whose adult needs may be so diverse? I argue that it can only be a curriculum which allows children to:
- gain a broad experience of mathematics;
- be challenged intellectually by mathematical ideas;
- celebrate success rather than failure in classrooms and exam rooms;
- gain access to the whole curriculum;
- see how maths is useful and relevant whatever their future lives;
- see that they can operate independently and collaboratively to solve problems.

A sound mathematics curriculum requires a study of mathematics which secures understanding and competence. *Using and applying* becomes a crucial Programme of Study because nowhere else in the mathematics curriculum is it so easy to find words and phrases that help the teacher identify what quality experiences might be like. The content contained within *number and algebra, shape and space and measures*, and *data handling and probability* are too focused on listing what has to be acquired in terms of knowledge and skills to be able to suggest **what the 'experience' of learning mathematics should be like**.

Chapter 6

Teaching and learning mathematics

Teaching styles and managing change

During 1995 and 1996 over what is a relatively short space of time, styles of teaching underwent a noticeable change in many schools. Some of the influencing factors were:

- larger classes;
- organising the teaching of children in ability groups at both Key Stages 1 and 2;
- the knock-on effect of the National Curriculum on long-term, medium-term and short-term planning, and the effect of this planning on teaching;
- OFSTED publications that have focused debate on the 'quality of teaching';
- school action plans written in response to key issues identified during school inspection.

Classroom practice and its central importance

When a coordinator is first appointed, whether this is to a new school or a change of responsibility within the existing school, many appointees need time to reflect on their own practice and ideally receive inservice development from LEA advisory staff, consultants and through participation on courses, e.g. GEST, funded TTA or Standards Fund. The coordinator's classroom practice lies at the heart of successful coordination of mathematics. It is an essential base on which to build the other work that is expected of a coordinator. It is also a most useful way of demonstrating to colleagues what the effective teaching of mathematics can achieve.

Many teachers dismiss their teaching as nothing out of the ordinary, and coordinators of mathematics are no exception to this habit. There needs to be a change of heart about this dismissiveness of professionalism. A richer and more complex range of discussions can take place when coordinators help colleagues to be objective and more celebratory about the skills they possess. In a climate where people are comfortable about discussing their strengths objectively, it's easier to identify and describe the factors that have influenced effectiveness. The climate is something that only the teachers themselves can create but there are some areas that are useful to work on. When you work with colleagues you can help them to be more comfortable about talking up their strengths by:

■ picking an individual child who has made good progress recently and looking closely at the child's achievements and identifying specific interventions that the teacher made which helped support the child;
■ focusing on something that the teacher has recently developed in their teaching and looking at why that development has come about;
■ writing a list of achievements over the last year;
■ using examples of children's work that have been 'levelled' and discussing why the work can't be assessed at the next level, and looking at what the teacher needs to do to give the child access to the next level;
■ making full use of appraisal to review their effectiveness and helping them to set achievable goals for the next year.

If good practice is to be nurtured, encouraging its spread can only be done in a climate where teachers can accept praise for effective teaching and are able to recognise and acknowledge for themselves, those parts of their teaching which are of high quality. This is an essential first stage if there is to be any constructive discussion about teaching effectiveness, e.g.:

- Why does our effectiveness in some curriculum areas often lag behind our effectiveness in other areas?
- What makes us feel de-skilled and prevents us from drawing on the skills we have?
- When we resist doing something the way a colleague does it, what is the source and nature of our resistance?
- How do we go about taking and using ideas given to us by colleagues? Do we acquire new skills in the most effective ways?

There are some very fixed ways of thinking and working in educational establishments and they often ignore the findings of most recent research or experience in other fields. For example, children and teachers can suffer stress in classrooms and there are lots of workshops and classes outside school that help people reduce stress, but very few teachers use breathing exercises, yoga or relaxation with their children in school: it's as if schools aren't allowed to be places where people can practice being healthy. In his highly pertinent book, Guy Claxton, (1997) looks at how we tackle problems in our lives and how limited some of the traditional ways of working and thinking are. An experimental psychologist, he draws upon really up-to-date research about brain function and uses it to look at how we can be creative in solving everyday problems.

It's difficult for teachers to know how effective they are. One reason is that part of the process of learning is to turn skills and techniques which are initially difficult, into processes which function automatically. As a consequence we forget what we were like as teachers a year, or five years ago. As we become more skilled in settling a class and preparing them for work, we don't need to explicitly remember how we do it: we just 'do it'. Routines are 'subordinated' in Gattegno's language, freeing our creative thinking for new or more complex tasks. Car driving is probably the best example of a complex set of skills which become automated on mastery. Making our routine behaviours more automatic leaves us free to direct our creative minds elsewhere — but leaves us less aware of how effective we are. Effective teaching requires us to draw on complex skills and intuition in very complex human interactions. As we develop as teachers, much of what was initially difficult becomes an easily managed routine, such as beginning and ending a lesson without great disruption, switching from talking to the whole class to getting children working in groups, etc. Having established some of these routines we just carry them out on most occasions but we are alert to unsatisfactory situations and when these arise, we can change the routine. Unless there is a need to modify our behaviour, both we and the children learn to follow the routine.

Having made the less important aspects of our teaching routines automatic, we are free to think more imaginatively about the more important parts of our work. However, some skills and teaching techniques that become routine may be undeveloped, inefficient and problematic both for experienced and inexperienced teachers alike. Routine practice has to be periodically examined. The coordinator has to regain access to knowledge about their teaching that they have previously subordinated. They have to rediscover their routine teaching styles if they are to have informed discussions with colleagues about effective teaching. They need to re-awaken their awareness of what they do, rather than what they *think* they do. In this way, awareness of one's own practice helps us create a climate of discussion that will be useful to colleagues. Each coordinator's own practice needs to become the renewed focus of their attention.

Raising the status of teachers begins with a celebration of the high level of skill and insight required to do the work. Claims of ordinariness have to be rejected as insufficiently analytical. Close examination of the particular classroom practice of individual teachers frequently provides valuable models for others to explore and adopt. For the inexperienced and newly qualified, access to a range of specific techniques is crucial if they are to remain constructively analytical about the quality of their work and sensitive to ways of improving it. One of the most useful outcomes of inservice support for the coordinator is the acquisition of a framework for describing and analysing classroom practice. This:

- supports the review and development of one's own classroom practice;
- helps the coordinator develop a language for discussing classroom practice with colleagues;
- eventually influences the whole staff, raising the quality of discussion about classroom practice throughout the whole school;
- allows the school's practice and policy to be much more effectively communicated to outside bodies such as parents, governors, newly appointed colleagues and inspectors.

Thinking skills and learning styles

There has been a lot of interest in learning styles over recent years. The results of research, much of it innovative, offers clear suggestions about ways to improve the classroom as a learning environment. A fascinating book by Bernice McCarthy (1987) provides a way of assessing preferred learning styles using ratings from questions that are mapped onto a target that divides learning styles into four broad categories. The results provide a basis for teachers to ask themselves how to present the knowledge and skills that are to be taught so that children with dominant styles can readily assimilate and comprehend the ideas.

Teaching thinking is not universally thought of as a good idea or a panacea. Michael Bonnet (1995) has argued that it can create problems. One of the supporters of teaching about thinking is Robert Fisher (1990). In his book *Teaching Children to Think*, he evaluates and analyses world-wide research into the teaching of thinking skills. Perhaps the most famous, original and controversial work, much of it related to helping children with learning difficulties, has been done by Reuven Feuerstein (1983). A very accessible and up-to-date discussion of Feuerstein's work of teaching intelligence and the notion of mediated learning, can be found in *Changing Children's Minds* by Sharron (1994). Some of the work of authors can lead straight to useful ways in which we can check up on our classrooms and what they offer children. Howard Gardner's work (1993) is a good example. Each of Gardner's 7 intelligences can be mapped against different types of maths activity. This serves as a useful check on:

■ the range of mathematical experiences available to children;

■ which types of learning style are being supported.

For teachers at Key Stage 1 it is often useful to start by drawing a picture of the classroom showing the different areas and the practical activities that are associated with each one. For Key Stage 2 teachers, a list of different activities is sometimes more useful.

It's clear that many children struggle to understand maths at different times in their lives. Two aspects of schooling that teachers have immediate influence over are; their own teaching style, and their classroom organisation. By reviewing and developing these, teachers can improve their effectiveness and have a dramatic impact on the success of learners. The ideas inherent in the theories of learning styles and the teaching of learning, emphasise the important influence on learning brought about by the way information is presented, explored and mediated by the teacher. We are not always aware of what we do in the classroom or what effect our teaching has on learning. Reviewing our ideas about learning styles and about teaching thinking, is a good place to start.

Blobs and links — a simple theory of learning

The work we do with children is inevitably based on our beliefs about learning and teaching. These are often hidden and swamped by the demands of solving immediate classroom problems. It is useful if coordinators can find ways to get teachers to articulate their beliefs about teaching and learning. In a confident group this will lead to discussions of the differences between different people's views and eventually to a more coherent philosophy between colleagues in a school. It has a unifying effect where individual beliefs are welcomed as contributing to the whole school. How do children learn the maths we teach them? What do colleagues understand of the learning process?

For many children and adults, difficulties with maths often include a failure to know *when* to use the skills and knowledge that have been painstakingly built up over years of schooling. At its crudest, a model of maths understanding is *blobs and links*. *Blobs* are knowledge that can be named: 'two halves make a quarter'; '180 degrees is the same as a right angle'. *Links* are connections that a learner can make between different blobs that have no immediately obvious connections: '❦, half, fifty-fifty, ten out of twenty, fifty out of a hundred, 50%, 5/10, two quarters'. *Links are knowledge* in the same way that *blobs are knowledge*. Indeed developing links is a sign of greater knowledge than knowledge of blobs alone. Knowing that 50% and two quarters can be used to refer to the same amount is only possible when children have certain meta-knowledge.

1 To think mathematically, they need to know the internal rules that govern the generation of each form. They need to know about percentages; about how to 'read' the squiggle %; and how fractions can be made to work.
2 They need to know how to convert one form into the other, or both into something else, into 4 eighths for example. They need to know how to compare different forms and how to verify that all three forms represent the same amount.

When teachers work *explicitly* with children on exposing the links, the extent of their knowledge about conversion and different ways of representing mathematical ideas is made much more accessible to both teacher and children. By explicitly showing how links are built up, e.g. by using concept maps, children become aware of the need to build the links themselves, and with help, they can begin to extend the linking process on their own. When they are given a chance to show they can make their own links, they also demonstrate that they have some understanding of the blobs that they are linking.

They may well know some blobs separately, intimately and thoroughly. However, being able to demonstrate this isolated knowledge doesn't provide the teacher with any evidence that the children know how to link the blobs. Children need to know how to draw potentially isolated facts into their network of knowledge, making new knowledge accessible and available for future use. Many people report that making links wasn't something that was taught at school but was more often left to chance. In consequence not only does mathematical flexibility and agility suffer but also the blobs that have been acquired may fade through under-use and poor access.

Teaching links without teaching blobs is not possible. Teaching blobs without teaching links is bad news for learners of maths. Imagining that learners will discover links if they are taught unconnected blobs of knowledge is wishful thinking of the most unhelpful and limiting kind. The layout of the mathematics National Curriculum is brilliant for identifying blobs, but pretty useless at helping teachers identify links. *Models of learning — tools for teaching*, by Bruce Joyce is a useful and very practical book in which he discusses a range of learning and teaching methods together with classroom examples across the curriculum subjects. Fortunately, *using and applying* has been retained in the latest National Curriculum revision. Despite being weakly structured it is nevertheless an important part of the curriculum. The coordinator can usefully review the effectiveness of the teaching of *using and applying* by focusing on the three strands:

- mathematical decision making;
- communicating;
- reasoning.

I've found it useful to view the *using and applying* Programme of Study as a description (if not a definition) of effective teaching and good practice. So, supporting the development of *using and applying* in the classroom can be easier to achieve if the focus is on the teacher's behaviour rather than the children's. A useful book by Christine Hopkins (1996) contains suggestions about ways of developing *using and applying*.

Whole school approaches to teaching and learning

Teachers regularly seek help from coordinators to solve their individual problems. Increasingly, coordinators will need to provide suggestions and solutions that ensure a greater unity of practice throughout the school. The introduction of the

National Curriculum and other recent changes in assessment and inspection have emphasised continuity and progression of the curriculum across classes and through the key stages. As a consequence teachers have to work closely together to unify the curriculum and ensure coherence of children's experience.

Many coordinators work hard to unify their school's practice by:

1   meeting groups of colleagues and helping them draw out the teaching implications of Programme of Study statements: e.g. *shape, space and measures* 3c 'use right angles, fractions of a turn and, later, degrees, to measure rotation, and use the associated language';

2   establishing ways of planning whereby teachers can assure themselves that the work suggested by the school's scheme of work meets the learning objectives that have been identified as appropriate for the children they are teaching;

3   helping teachers to improve their effectiveness by providing a wide choice of activities that they can draw on when planning work for children around a learning objective;

4   helping colleagues tackle the ideas expressed in the learning objectives in a number of varied ways;

5   helping colleagues to teach in more effective ways by working alongside them in classrooms;

6   by using small amounts of non-contact time to look in depth at particular aspects of current practice, e.g. visiting classrooms to help colleagues develop similar routines for monitoring children during mathematical activity;

7   exploring with groups of colleagues the pre-requisite knowledge and skills that are needed to tackle specific work in maths, e.g. what knowledge and skills do we need to be able to draw on when tackling a division problem like $36 \div 7$ or when finding the next number in a sequence like 0, 1, 3, 6, 10, . . . generated by the 'handshake problem'. (One person alone cannot shake another's hand. When two people meet and shake hands once, we can say that this counts as one handshake (although, intriguingly, both people may claim to have 'shaken someone else's hand today' which can lead us to argue for a result of 2)! If three people meet and shake each other's hand once, then we can argue the total number of handshakes is 3, and so on. What can we say about the situation that occurs when everyone in the class shakes hands with everyone else in this way?);

8   providing a common structure for teachers to plan, implement, assess and evaluate the teaching and learning that takes place in their classroom.

We know that for children to understand mathematics and perform well, they need to be able, to:

- independently recognise links between previous knowledge and the current lesson;
- practise skills and consolidate their recall of basic facts;
- fix new knowledge efficiently;
- explain, discuss and describe their work confidently and eloquently;
- be open and responsive to a range of teaching styles.

Most children are unlikely to do this consistently without support and training. Success is more common in lessons where teachers expressly point these qualities out to children and make their acquisition an explicit part of the lesson.

One of the most significant characteristics of good mathematics teaching is that it is accompanied by a great deal of discussion that is led by the teacher but not exclusively teacher dominated. In contrast, little of the time is spent discussing behaviour, control and discipline, or classroom routine. The more the teacher can help children to express themselves through mathematical discussion, the more effective the learning is likely to be and the easier it is for misconceptions to be brought out in the open and explored. A second feature of good maths teaching is that effective teaching and learning occur when the teacher, at the beginning of the lesson, explicitly describes to the children the purpose of the mathematics work they are about to carry out.

Successful maths lessons have a number of characteristics by which they can be recognised:

- the children are told at the beginning what they are likely to learn during the lesson and what skills they will develop. They know at the outset what they have to do well in order to have a successful lesson;
- the lessons are exciting and engaging to children;
- teachers often make lessons puzzling, enjoyable and mystifying;
- many lessons start from other curriculum areas, like reading the story of Noah's Ark, or studying the locality;
- many lessons are specifically about mathematics for its own sake;

- there are periods of genuine discussion, along with effective questioning and quiet times for thinking and practising;
- teachers don't imply or suggest that children are stupid if they don't have immediate answers;
- the fastest thinkers aren't the only ones who are celebrated. Being a slow thinker is OK too and so is not being sure;
- it's OK to make mistakes, in fact mistakes are often enthusiastically taken up by teachers and children as interesting things to explore further, and making mistakes is seen as natural, something we all do and not a sign of stupidity;
- thoroughness and care are encouraged, even when this means that some children need to spend much longer on producing careful work than others do;
- alternative ways of working are actively encouraged, but inefficient methods are identified and more efficient ways demonstrated;
- all children are expected to achieve some if not all of the objectives of the lesson.

In many schools the coordinator is not in a position to know that this is going on in all classes. In only one primary school that I've visited recently have all the coordinators received release time on a regular weekly basis to teach alongside colleagues for part of each week to monitor teaching directly. In most schools monitoring teaching is done indirectly for the most part. Schools are reviewing the way they use their budgets, but many schools are insufficiently financed to do the job properly. Nevertheless, coordinators need to have strategies to monitor the teaching and this can be done through discussion and informal chats as well as through the use of formal procedures.

There are disruptive external forces which are working against improving curriculum provision. Some of these disruptions stem directly from the way in which SATs results are used and league tables published: some are directly related to the way the National Curriculum has been constructed and written. It is clear that as they stand, the mathematics Programmes of Study cannot nurture good quality teaching by themselves. They are too terse, offer little guidance and they lack an appropriate structure to emphasise useful links between ideas and skills contained in the

Martin Hughes' research findings have been taken up by many teachers interested in 'emergent mathematics' and many of his experimental activities have been adapted by teachers as activities for children in the early years. With 4 and 5-year-olds, for example, this could involve asking them to draw or write something that would help them remember how many cubes they've put into a yoghurt pot. 'How many cubes have you put in your pot?' (Three). 'Show me. Yes. OK. Watch. I'm going to put a lid on the pot so you can't see the cubes. Tomorrow I'm going to ask you how many cubes are in the pot. You'll have to tell me, before you look. Can you think of something that you could draw on the lid to help you remember? What could you draw on the lid so that in the morning, when you come in, you can see straightaway, how many cubes are in your pot? Can you draw something that will tell you?'

Not only does this provide a purpose for recording. If they have a pot each, it invites a creative response from each child and an opportunity, the following day, for a group of children to compare ideas. Some may draw one house for each cube, others may use tally strokes, some may write numerals or dots, some will invent a unique symbol. As teachers, we can gain considerable insight into children's thinking by inviting them to solve problems using what they already know, rather than something we've recently taught them.

different parts of the curriculum. The overall effect of the structural arrangement of many of the elements of the National Curriculum is to fragment the mathematics curriculum and push teachers towards providing short-term, disconnected activities followed by an immediate test to assess the children's retention of information over a short period. This is depressingly evident in many Year 2 and Year 6 classes and is an immediate consequence of having to ensure that the school's position in the league tables is as high as possible, and this of course has to be done by getting children to score as highly as possible on SATs. The effect in some schools is to reduce Key Stage 2 from four years to three with Year 6 children spending the year preoccupied with revision: in many ways an understandable, pragmatic response by teachers caught in the turmoil caused by half-baked political ideology.

Can research in psychology help?

Margaret Donaldson has become one of the best known and influential psychologists writing in Britain. *Children's Minds*, (Donaldson, 1978) has probably been read by more British teachers than any other text written by a psychologist in recent years. Her later book, *Human Minds* (1992) develops many of her earlier ideas and contains useful insights into learning in the early years. Martin Hughes (1984) made an important contribution to thinking about mathematics teaching and learning in his book *Children and Number*. In it, Hughes discusses young children's invention and use of number signs and symbols.

It's very important to ask whether psychological research about behaviour and attitudes can help us to develop classrooms as places where mathematics can be learned more effectively. Does what we know from recent psychological research about learning get translated into good practice in the classroom? Unfortunately it doesn't seem that this is always the case. In his book, *Being a Teacher*, Guy Claxton (1989) says the following about children's views of themselves as being either 'bright' or 'dim'.

❛ . . . *if you believe that 'ability' means 'worth' (and therefore that 'lack of ability' threatens shame or rejection from others)* and *that ability is fixed, then you are likely to find yourself in survival-mode when you meet or anticipate obstacles and problems. But if you* either *don't buy the idea that you've got to be smart all the time to be loveable,* or *you think that it is possible to get smarter if you try, then there is less to be afraid of, and more to be gained, from grappling with tough tasks than from avoiding them. [This unhelpful theory] . . . of ability is actually compounded of three sub-beliefs. The first, . . . is the idea that ability is* immutable: *if you are bright you will stay bright; if you are dim you will stay dim. The second says that ability is* pervasive: *if you are bright in one subject you will, all things being equal, be bright . . . in other subjects and your 'ability level' in school reflects your 'ability level' outside. The third says that ability is* monolithic: *that it is an integral, unitary quality and not compounded of a variety of constituents. . . . These beliefs are demonstrably false and now widely known to be so by many teachers. [but they often] . . . remain dissolved in the way teachers inadvertently talk to pupils, to each other, and write reports. If teachers were not unconsciously wedded to these assumptions they would not be as frequently disconcerted as they are by their pupils' variability . . .* (pp. 179–80)

Claxton's *mastery-mode* is characterised by phrases like: 'when the going gets tough the tough get going'. If you're in 'survival-mode' or you are 'helpless-prone' then you daren't risk being wrong or showing yourself up by not succeeding at a task. You will tend to avoid work that looks difficult, you won't take risks, you may copy other people's behaviour if they are the ones who are usually clever, you may constantly seek reassurance.

Putting children into survival-mode or mastery-mode is a function of teaching and has more to do with classroom atmosphere than a child's 'personality'. What Claxton is suggesting is, if we can change the classroom into a learning environment where it is OK to make mistakes, where being stuck is an interesting phenomena to be puzzled and excited about, rather than something which invites ridicule, scorn or frustration from the teacher, most children will change from *helpless-prone* to *mastery-mode*. It is personal worth that makes the difference. In a classroom where children feel a sense of personal worth that is quite distinct from their ability to 'do the work they've been given' then they are more likely to attack problems of all sorts with enthusiasm and interest. In a classroom where it's OK not to know the answer, where it's OK to ask the teacher a question, where it's OK to get important things wrong, it's worth the risk to get stuck in. Where there is little sign of being regarded as worthy, and especially where 'worthiness' is linked to getting things right, being quick, knowing the answer, not making errors, then it can easily become too risky to tackle problems.

If success brings comments like 'well done, you're clever' then not succeeding is more likely to be seen as being stupid. The point is that even when they are very young, children fall into two distinct groups in their views about cleverness. One group sees it as fixed: either you are clever or you are not. If you hold this view, by the time you've started school or pretty soon afterwards, you will probably have decided which group you think you belong to. If, however, you see cleverness as malleable and changeable, you tend to see tackling problems as a way of getting brighter. The problem with classrooms is that getting things finished, getting things right, being neat, being fast are all highly valued. In the end these are the qualities that teachers really (seem to) want. If you regard cleverness as fixed then you might as well stop trying immediately because, obviously, it's a waste of time trying to be what you're not. If you see cleverness as malleable, and getting stuck in means you might solve a problem and solving a problem means you're now a little bit brighter, then getting stuck in is going to pay off.

Many young children see the world in these terms very soon after starting school. Teachers influence these views and in mathematics, often reinforce views which nudge children towards a *helpless-prone*, survival mode. This often becomes very apparent when teachers introduce investigations and activities designed to encourage *using and applying*. If the classroom encourages helpless-prone behaviour, then a sudden switch to problem solving and investigations creates the most risky situations for those who are in *survival-mode*. If the teacher creates a classroom where the children are in survival-mode, and the teacher is also in the same mode because teaching maths is seen as very risky, something that they are not good at, then the introduction of open-ended problem solving and investigations is going to be enormously risky behaviour, to be avoided at all costs!

Chapter 7

Parents and mathematics

Ensuring parents feel involved in their children's learning of mathematics can result in big improvements in their children's achievements. Many schools have excellent relationships with parents and have found valuable ways to communicate with them about mathematics. Many parents help in classrooms and attend parents' evenings. Maths days, family maths trails, homework and maths games afternoons can all help to demystify what for many parents can still be one of the most mystifying aspects of their children's school life. It's not the maths that puzzles people; it's the assumption, made by many parents, that it's all taught differently these days.

Things for the mathematics coordinator to consider when working with parents are listed in Figure 7.1.

One view that has been carefully nurtured in some sections of the national press suggest that parents are generally dissatisfied with schools. This view then allowed easy development of the description of parents as 'consumers'. In the late 1980s, consumer choice was a continuing theme in many areas of peoples' lives. The Education White Paper (1992) *Choice and Diversity: A New Framework for Schools* used this froth of supposed widespread dissatisfaction to nurture a climate of attacks on teaching and to promote an apparent increase in 'parental choice'.

Working with parents	What and how are we doing?
Discussion and agreement with the staff. Are we agreed about what we should be doing for and with parents?	
How are we building up relationships with parents who cannot easily get to the school to see us?	
Are we getting the information we need to and from parents?	
Is our policy for involving parents with mathematics coherent and being followed?	
How do we handle parent's concerns about their child's progress in maths or their desire to help them at home? Is every one clear about our policy?	
How inviting is the school to parents? If I were to walk through the school with a parent what would they see/say?	
How do we discuss maths with parents? Is there a simple set of suggestions that colleagues would welcome?	
Do we know individual parents' hopes for their children? Would it be useful to note them down? Do they match the school's aims for the children?	
Do parents understand our jargon? Have we really eradicated it from parents' information so we can communicate clearly and unambiguously?	
Do parents understand where we stand on the learning of basic facts and skills; the use of calculators; the value of investigations? Do we present a coherent picture or do parents get different messages from different staff — including support staff?	
Are parents clear about what we expect children to record in maths?	
Are we doing the best we can to get parents involved in maths?	

FIG 7.1
Working with parents

© Falmer Press Ltd

Suggestion

As a coordinator are you clear about what parents want from the school in terms of maths? Do you think you're providing what they want and need as well as what is required by law? What successes have you had in keeping parents informed? Would a quick chat at the school gate confirm what you believe? Are there further opportunities to promote your subject with parents without expending too much energy? You could review the specific things you offer parents and review why they are successful. You are then in a position to ask yourself and others what else could be done and what would be the specific purpose of any new venture?

It is important to emphasise that there is research evidence to challenge the view that parents are dissatisfied with their children's education. In *Parents and their children's schools*, for example, Martin Hughes and others looked at parental satisfaction.

> *Another assumption underlying the (government's) reforms is that parents are deeply dissatisfied with their children's schools, and particularly with the standards which prevail. Our research provides little evidence to support this. Each year the vast majority of parents said they were happy with their child's school and that the teachers were doing a good job. Over three quarters of the parents were happy with their children's progress in English and maths ... These figures do not suggest widespread dissatisfaction amongst parents; rather they indicate general approval of schools as they are at present, and a significant appreciation of the job which teachers are doing.*
>
> (Hughes et al., 1994)

Most parents and carers want to help their children do as well as they can and in mathematics it is still not easy to communicate how they can help. Parents are often more anxious about 'doing the right thing' in maths than in most other subjects and children seem to be more likely to resist help from parents, 'My teacher doesn't do it like that!' Many coordinators have produced jargon-free booklets for parents that give explicit guidance about how they can help. One booklet I came across recently from a school in Oxfordshire, set out clearly how the school teaches children to add and subtract. The school doesn't use decomposition for subtraction instead it favours a written layout that mirrors the mental methods taught in the school. So in both mental and written calculations, children are taught to start with the tens and then do the units. The booklet is produced both to show parents how written addition and subtraction methods are taught but is also an invitation to parents to help their children.

You may be reviewing issues related to homework. If you are, you will need to consider what your intentions are in developing or changing your homework policy. Your main goal might be for all children to have an opportunity to continue exploring ideas at home with their parents. If the point of maths homework is to involve parents, or at least show them the kinds of things their children do in school, and not just to provide the simplest and most routine activities of learning tables or doing extra 'sums', then careful thought needs to be given to a range of activities suitable for home use. The early years magazine published by the BBC has a lot of useful ideas and an attractive format. As you acquire good ways of developing home-based activities, homework suggestions could be added to the scheme of work so that teachers can think about home-school links as they do their medium-term planning.

One of the most influential projects that has been developed is IMPACT, (Maths with Parents and Children and Teachers). It now involves hundreds of schools and the activities are now published by Scholastic. The IMPACT director Ruth Merttens and others, provide Inset and parents' evenings to launch IMPACT in schools and some LEAs have bought into the project on behalf of their schools. IMPACT has tended to provoke strong responses. Some teachers see it as taking too much time away from other maths work in school as they deal with the results of the work that (some) children have done at home. Other teachers enthusiastically welcome the work that children have done at home and take great care to build the IMPACT activities into their other classroom teaching. The directors of IMPACT argue their case in their book, *Partnership in Maths: Parents and Schools, The IMPACT Project*, (Merttens and Vass, 1993). The book draws on a number of case studies, written by parents, teachers, and others who reflect on introducing and using the project to promote mathematics and parental involvement. The best results, not surprisingly, are achieved where a committed school convinces parents before starting up the project and both groups give time and enthusiasm to the children and their activities each week.

For coordinators who have taken on or been given a specific brief to extend and develop the involvement of parents in mathematics, there is a valuable resource provided in a document that has become known as the 'PrIME File' (1992). It contains one complete unit (Unit H) on involving parents in mathematics. The unit provides valuable advice and detailed practical guidance on a range of issues such as: devising a questionnaire to obtain parental views; planning, organising and running a parents' meeting about maths; leading a parents' workshop, with suggestions for activities; planning a workshop for children and parents; ideas about maths at home; the role of parents in the classroom; building a maths games library. *Mathematics in ILEA Primary Schools: A Handbook for the Mathematics Coordinator* (ILEA, 1988) has a useful chapter devoted to working with parents and a much slimmer volume, but one containing useful advice and practical suggestions is the Mathematical Association's *Sharing Mathematics with Parents: Planning school-based events* (1987), which deals with ideas useful to both primary and secondary schools.

Chapter 8   Professional development

I've always taken the view that being a coordinator puts you into a middle management role within the primary school management team. How can the coordinator contribute to the management of staff development? What is the point of staff development? This seems a trivial question but it is surprising that even some of the best schools haven't got a clear picture of the *purpose* of staff development and, as a result, the overall effect doesn't have the impact that it should have.

One of the main purposes of providing schools in our society is to provide children with unique experiences, experiences that they can't get anywhere else. It is to provide them with real opportunities for personal development, both intellectually and socially. The most influential factor in all of this is the teaching they receive. The quality of the teaching is the main influence on the quality of the learning environment in which the children find themselves. It follows from this argument that staff development must lead to improvements in children's learning and in the standards they achieve. Standards can be interpreted broadly to include; behaviour, emotional maturity, independence, love of learning, collaboration, as well as intellectual development and knowledge and understanding of the subject. Looking at basic principles and beliefs gives a direction to staff development and a way of evaluating it.

So, the fundamental question to ask yourself as a subject leader is whether the staff development leads directly to improvements in standards. Are improvements clearly evident or just wished for? The coordinator is not necessarily responsible for deciding how and what staff development takes place. As a middle manager, the responsibility is to pass information and your professional opinion to both the SMT and to your teaching colleagues. For individual colleagues who are class teachers, the results of effective staff development should include:

- increased subject knowledge, understanding and expertise;
- increased confidence and enjoyment in teaching the subject;
- development of relationships and increased understanding of the needs of others, so that learning mathematics is a humanising experience in school;
- developments in classroom organisation and management;
- increased diversity and quality in the range of teaching styles teachers can employ;
- suggestions for teachers to increase excitement, puzzlement and enthusiasm in children as they learn mathematics;
- more varied and effective ways of managing children, including the promotion of children's increased independence, self and peer review and self-assessment.

One of the more significant consequences of the introduction of a National Curriculum is that staff in the most successful schools work much more closely together as a collaborative team. It's now very unlikely that teachers who work in isolation can contribute to school development. Isolation impedes the improvement of school effectiveness. Ensuring good relationships and developing collaborative working environments is often high on women's agendas for achieving job satisfaction and is a way of working that many men find difficult to achieve without support. It is unsurprising that one of the characteristics of many of the more successful schools is the high percentage of women in leadership roles. Close team work is the best way of ensuring continuity and progression in the mathematics curriculum throughout the school.

1 Effective leadership is vital. Effective leaders have a positive self image. They are not so easily tempted by the power of their job to use the leadership position to confer importance on themselves over others.

2 Leaders use their position to ensure that others are confident in their work and feel free to express ideas and opinions. Dissident views don't easily threaten a team that wants to stay together.

3 Leaders show direction. Team members show confidence. There is a measure of agreement about the generally accepted direction that the school is moving.

4 In response to the vision of the school, the team forms organisational arrangements that support everybody in meeting the demands of their respective roles. The test of good organisational arrangements is that people usually feel comfortable; ways of working seem natural, and the team tries to find ways to make it easier to do what needs to be done.

5 The effective leader brings unresolved problems to the group and seeks help and advice as well as giving it. The team expects affective responses to be overt: expressions of hope, anxiety, elation and concern, etc. naturally arise in the team's conversation.

There are some essential components to good professional development, all of which are clearly evident in effective schools.

1 Individual teachers get regular (if not frequent) staff development opportunities *of their own choosing.*

2 Individual teachers take up opportunities for professional development that the *school* needs them to take — and they take it up because they know why the school needs it.

3 The whole team gets staff development as a group, sometimes from individual 'experts' from within the team and sometimes from outsiders who join the group for a period of time.

4 Time (and money) is spent making sure that the maximum benefit is derived from staff development through dissemination.

The subject leader plays a key role in ensuring that these four ways of providing staff development all function effectively within the existing budget. You then need to ensure that effective staff development in mathematics is more likely, rather than less likely to happen. It's useful to ask yourself:

■ Do I regularly collect other peoples' ideas and talk to colleagues about what they think should happen as far as mathematics is concerned? Do I hear what they say?

■ Do I let people know what's available and what's possible?

■ Do I contribute to the development of non-teaching colleagues and parent volunteers in their work with children; e.g. by giving learning support staff and parent volunteers a written list of suitable open questions to ask children when they supervise activities; do I help dinner supervisors to support mathematical activity in the playground by helping children to play games like hopscotch?

■ Do I organise meetings so that individuals' expertise is a source of staff development for others?

■ Are the needs of the school being met by the current arrangement for professional development?

■ Do I share my thoughts with the SMT about what I think is the best way of balancing the schools' needs against the needs of individuals?

■ Is there effective mentoring for newly appointed staff, so they get a clear sense of our aims — know what we do in our mathematics teaching?

Frequently, the coordinator's role in staff development is to assess and communicate the school's needs in relation to mathematics and advise the SMT. The final decision is likely to be taken by the head when all coordinators have communicated what the needs are in their respective subjects. It is vital that the SMT get good information to guide them as they prioritise needs against a finite budget.

The result of a good flow of information throughout the school leads to the subject leader and the SMT being able to:

■ tackle the most important things first;

■ match school and individual needs;

■ identify the people who will be involved and the limit of their responsibility;

■ calculate the cost of each staff development venture;

■ specify a method by which the benefit of each initiative will be evaluated.

These elements should all be present in the SDP and this is discussed in detail in the next section.

The subject leader's full participation in the whole process is vital if the quality of provision in mathematics is going to improve.

The subject leader's own development

It's important to find a good balance between supporting colleagues and ensuring appropriate support for yourself. There are likely to be many colleagues who are really effective in the classroom as far as mathematics is concerned and they seldom get an opportunity to go on courses. The initiative in the GEST 1997–98 budget that requires 40 per cent of the expenditure on courses to go to mathematics has provided an opportunity for some of the best teachers to have their needs recognised. There is also scope, if LEAs and HE institutions have so chosen, to offer courses for those teachers who are not confident about teaching maths. It is vital that coordinators balance their own needs against those of colleagues and, where the need arises, ensure that they themselves take the opportunity for professional development.

Looking to the future, the TTA is planning to offer courses which will provide a qualification for subject leaders. The consultation paper published by the TTA in November 1996 had some serious shortcomings and was very much tarnished with the political mood of the time. Singularly, it failed to address the issue that many subject leaders have responsibility for two and sometimes three curriculum areas and that vast numbers of them in primary schools get absolutely no financial reward for these extra duties and responsibilities. Having said this, if the right balance is struck then a new professional award that prepares subject leaders for the work and provides appropriate training time, will be an improvement over current levels of support. If however, the award is established as part of an inspection process that is designed to check up on teachers, then it needs to be firmly rejected. In the consultation paper the principles on which the qualification should be based were listed as being:

- rooted in school improvement and build on the best practice found inside and outside education;
- based on an agreed set of national standards for subject leaders;
- rigorous enough to ensure only those who have the necessary skills, abilities, knowledge and understanding gain the qualification;
- designed to take account of existing proven skills and achievements;
- available to aspiring and existing subject leaders.

It's likely that assessment would include a range of things, some of which are clearly the responsibility of the primary subject leader, e.g. to evaluate resources, but also including some things which are not the current responsibility of a primary teacher. The qualification may well be for primary and secondary teachers but some of the criteria for assessment outlined in the draft paper are traditionally the preserve of the primary head and SMT rather than something the subject coordinator would have control over. They include for example:

- the ability to develop and write a clear vision plan for subject development within the school;
- to identify the school's strengths and weaknesses in supporting the teaching of the subject;
- to accurately record pupil achievement and set clear and achievable targets for improvement;
- to observe teachers teaching and identify key strengths and weaknesses across a range of teaching styles and to set challenging but realistic targets for improvement.

For a primary subject leader with responsibility for two or three subject areas, being paid no extra remuneration and working in a school with only enough money to cover current staffing costs and no scope for paying for release time from the classroom, it's hard to see how some of these requirements might be met: always assuming teachers want to take on an inspectorial role in colleagues' classrooms.

There are many good things likely to come out of a qualification for subject leaders. A course should provide:

- an opportunity for professional development leading to financial reward for extra responsibility;
- a clear sense of promotion and a positive advancement in professional status;
- a consolidation of professional status for all teachers within primary schools;
- a simple and effective means of raising standards by helping subject leaders to more effectively support teachers.

Professional development and the school development plan

In order to ensure good value for the money spent, it is crucial that the School Development Plan (SDP) is used to publicly identify the priorities for the major expenditure on professional development. A balance has to be struck between the need of the school as a corporate body and the needs of the individuals, both teaching and non-teaching staff who work there. The SDP contains the aspirations of the governors, head and staff for the impending developments that are seen as the essential next steps for the school. As far as possible, the aspirations for development of the mathematics curriculum over the period covered by the SDP, will emerge as budgeted plans for action — hopefully after full discussion and agreement.

There has been a steady rise in the number of schools that allocate money in their SDP for releasing teachers, often the subject specialist, to carry out very precise tasks relating to the monitoring of the subject through the school and for creating opportunities for the subject specialist to work alongside other teachers for their mutual development. Whilst great opportunities for professional development derive from sending people out of school, it is very evident that some of the most successful developments come from tapping the enormous potential within schools and particularly within clusters of schools. For example, in

> Great strides are being made by closely targeting the work of subject specialists and releasing them for highly focused work. As one infant school head said to me; 'This is the third year that we've been releasing subject specialists to do curriculum development work. We thought we were focused three years ago, but after developing our practice during this period, we can now set ourselves very specific targets that we know are achievable and which feed immediately into our corporate knowledge of the current state of health of each curriculum subject in the school.'

Birmingham and elsewhere, Catholic primary schools regularly meet to share subject expertise as well as tackling other common issues.

Opportunities through GEST (Grants For Education Support and Training) currently funded by the DfEE but likely to become the responsibility of the TTA, or hopefully a General Teaching Council, provide courses for subject specialists to update and develop their subject expertise. Some of the money is available for generic courses for coordinators of subjects and curriculum coordinators, who, in many schools, have an over arching responsibility for curriculum coordination though with no specific subject responsibility. Details about places for GEST-funded courses are usually contained in LEA circulars to schools. Places are limited and LEAs often look at the whole school and its SDP when allocating places. HE institutions often provide GEST courses and are keen to provide other courses too. It's useful to keep contact with your local HE institution and suggest courses that you need as well as looking at what is advertised.

The grants being made available to schools by the TTA (Teacher Training Agency) to support teachers researching in their own schools is a relatively small but important source of funding for whole school development and the professional development of individual teachers. Reports of the work already carried out make interesting reading.

The work of the Numeracy Centres currently being funded by the government are likely to thrive, at least for a while, and the results of their work will pose major questions about the content, structure and time allocation for a 'new National Curriculum' that will inevitably be introduced before long. The Numeracy Centre curriculum programme seems to be expecting about five hours of work per week per class to be devoted to the mathematical activities they provide, in addition to any other work in mathematics that the class normally does. A government expectation to follow such a curriculum would demand major changes to the curriculum that is currently provided in primary schools. Where the work for the centres will lead is currently unclear, but professional development of subject leaders in maths is essential if there is to be an informed debate about changes to the mathematics curriculum of primary schools.

Subject leaders will increasingly be expected to demonstrate a knowledge of recent research, not only in the way children learn mathematics but also into the effectiveness of different teaching styles, particularly those recently referred to in public debate. It is crucial that teacher-generated research on what is found to be effective in schools in Britain, forms part of the debate on how to improve the teaching of mathematics through the development of teaching styles. Most schools have a bookshelf for staff that includes a good range of professional literature and the mathematics coordinator needs to check the range and quality to ensure there is a good selection available. A wide range of literature is listed in this handbook and this can be a starting point.

A strengthening of the teacher's role as a skilled professional, ironically comes about partly as a result of the work of OFSTED which Tim Brighouse as described as 'imposing a reign of terror on schools'. However inappropriate some aspects of the inspection process may be, the detail of inspections points clearly to a specialist professional body rather than continuing to cultivate the unskilled image that was promoted in recent years — where teachers were caricatured by John Major as a group that apparently did no more than an untrained 'mum's army' could accomplish. Recent changes have thrown into sharp relief the range and depth of the professional aspects of teachers' work.

Unfortunately, in our culture, high status is preferred on specialists whose work is unusual, skilful and to which there is some mystery associated. For years, teacher's have trod another route, to be open and approachable especially to parents and other professionals. The demystification of teaching as a profession over recent decades has been a factor in the demotion of teachers and has cost them a great deal in terms of status and salary; as well as personal and professional respect. An increase in professional distancing from other groups may be a necessary step to take. Professional development can lead not only to increased expertise and the higher educational standards that we all seek, but also to an enhanced status as the skills and expertise are increasingly acknowledged for what they are.

Working with colleagues

Schools are highly complex social settings. A sociological perspective suggests it is useful to be able to look at the setting as well as the part one plays in it. What we see as our role when working with colleagues will be determined by deeply held beliefs (Figure 8.1). It is important to explore how our beliefs influence our behaviour, particularly where being a subject leader includes working closely with colleagues. Are we clear what is directing and motivating our work? Who are we doing it for? What ideas are we attached to?

Some of the work that you do with colleagues will inevitably change both your own views and behaviour as well those of colleagues. Not all change is: comfortable, anticipated, welcome, pleasant, necessary, or appropriate. In his book *Being a Teacher: A Positive Approach to Change and Stress*, Guy Claxton, who is an experimental psychologist by training, identifies a number of stages and their accompanying feelings which he argues are involved in the process of change, (Claxton, 1989, pp. 120–21). The first and fourth columns in the following Figure 8.2, are my additions to Claxton's list. The whole table is an invitation to identify a change or a development and monitor yourself to 'see where you are'. My reading of Claxton is that all his stages are normal human responses; all are likely from time to time and each plays a part in the creative process of personal adjustment. Some stages will certainly feel less pleasant than others. Unfortunately in our society, bad feelings are often equated with the need for avoidance — and avoidance can lead to a consequent loss of valuable experience. Learning to stay with bad feelings can be very helpful, not only in teaching. Using the table for self-assessment, should raise your awareness of the positions that colleagues occupy as they manage changes; including those that you are putting into operation in mathematics.

Working with colleagues	How is it going? Can I spot where we're:		
	Strong	**Neutral**	**Weak**
What support and guidance is available for new colleagues and especially NQTs? What do **they** say?			
How well do colleagues understand the maths policy and the SoW? What other support would they like?			
How well do colleagues know and use the resources for maths?			
How well do colleagues use day-to-day assessment to shape their next bit of planning? How good are we at making opportunities for assessment through direct, focused classroom observation?			
What do they know about summative assessment processes, the record-keeping procedures and the marking policy? Do they need help to put plans into action?			
What am I doing to help colleagues prepare for their teaching? Do they get sufficient help in: selecting suitable activities, broadening their teaching styles, ensuring they provide adequate practical work, getting the most out of investigations and problem solving?			
How well do we monitor children's progress?			
Are colleagues making the best use of space, furniture and resources in their teaching areas?			
How well am I helping them develop the children's ability to work independently and collaboratively?			
What is the quality of display like throughout the school? Is it stimulating, inviting, touchable, interactive, current? How does it compare with other displays? Are there any links being made between maths and other subjects? Any evidence of maths being used **in** other subject displays?			
How good am I at circulating information, keeping people informed, providing interesting articles and clips from TES, other journals?			
What are the resources like? How well are they stored? Is storage and accessibility as good as in science, D&T, geography?			
Do non-teaching staff feel supported? Do I talk to them regularly to discuss their maths work load?			
Do I know the individual children who experience difficulties through the school? Could I find ways to get to know them better? Is there scope for an after-school club?			
Do I know the really able children? Do they stand out? Do they and their teachers feel supported?			
How well am I supporting colleagues by working with them in their rooms?			
Do I have a really broad repertoire of ways of working with individual children? Am I passing on my skills and knowledge to teaching and learning support colleagues?			
How effective are our discussion groups? Do we use a variety of styles to meet different needs and situations?			
How good am I at leading the team? Can I let them have their say and deviate from what I've planned? Can I be firm and ensure we get through important business and stick to what we've agreed? Do I start and finish on time? Do I respect other peoples' needs to have other priorities?			
Am I receptive to other peoples' ideas? How do I respond to things I don't agree with? Do colleagues agree this is how I am?			
How overburdening are our record-keeping systems? Do they really represent the minimum effort for the maximum effect? How often are we rewriting information that's already stored elsewhere in another format? What proportion of the information we produce and store is useful and to whom?			
Do colleagues meet and plan together regularly? As much as they want? How can I ease their workload, ease what's preventing them from achieving what they want?			
How well do I delegate tasks? Where are the opportunities to improve my ways of managing?			

FIG 8.1
Working with colleagues

Current changes and development	Stage	Feeling	Reasons for the feeling?
	Entrenchment	Uninterested, dismissive	
	Opposition	Argumentative, irritated, resistant	
	Possibility	Doubtful, sceptical, private, wondering	
	Dabbling	Uncommitted, interested, 'give it a go'	
	Agreement	Acceptant, 'like the idea'	
	Commitment	Enthusiastic, hopeful, talkative	
	Clarification	Puzzling, 'what does it really mean/involve?'	
	Introspection	Self-questioning, self-doubt, 'what have I been doing?'	
	Planning	Innovative, 'what can I try out?'	
	Experimentation	Nervous, feeling 'odd', excited	
	Reaction	Surprised, disappointed	
	Deflation	Disheartened, second thoughts, 'stuff it!'	
	Projection	Angry, blaming, betrayed	
	Reappraisal	Objective, 'sense of proportion', 'not so simple, but . . .'	
	Recuperation	Recharged, encouraged, 'feeling better'	
	Reaffirmation	Persistent, more realistic, more solid commitment	
	Extension	Inconsistent, fragmented, double standards	
	Evangelism	Preaching, over-enthusiastic, bumptious	
	Limitation	Judicious, perceiving limits of new approach	
	Consolidation	Confident, integrated, 'I've really got it'	
	Permeation	'I'm different', flexible, creative	

FIG 8.2
Monitoring change and development

A recent book edited by Paul Croll (1996) examines the way in which teachers respond to change. The book is a result of a research project called Primary Assessment, Curriculum and Experience (PACE). It looks closely at the experiences of teachers as they implemented the National Curriculum. Part of the data was collected through extensive interviews where teachers talked about the changes they experienced as the National Curriculum arrived and went through its various revisions.

A chapter written by Marilyn Osborn tells the story of two infant teachers in the same school both with over twenty years' experience. They fared very differently and Osborn describes what she calls a typology of teacher response to change. This is something that can prove useful in working with colleagues. Teachers have experienced several years of non-negotiated change to their work in education. Externally enforced change provokes different responses in different people. Many see teaching as a vocation and dedicate their work to the children in their classes. Those teachers who see externally enforced changes as threatening their relationship with children and undermining the purpose of education are likely to suffer what Nias (1993) describes as bereavement, and mourn the loss of opportunity to work according to their beliefs. It is no overstatement to describe some peoples' feelings in this way. The challenge is to recognise that the emotional context is as much an influence on ability to work professionally as any other factor — like subject knowledge. This is the learning context in which coordinators find their colleagues operating. Part of the skill of working with colleagues is to find ways to work constructively with all members of the school team.

If we are to take working with colleagues seriously, then there are three things we would do well to consider.
1 Understand that change is endemic and we are part of it.
2 Understand that we can influence others, that we should take responsibility for our actions but we are not responsible for the actions that others take.
3 That by understanding peoples' responses to change we can work more closely and more appropriately with them.

Perhaps helping them to use change more creatively for professional growth.

Marilyn Osborn (1996) lists five types of response to change.

Compliance: acceptance of the imposed changes and adjustment of teachers' professional ideology accordingly, so that greater central control is perceived as acceptable, or even desirable.

Incorporation: appearing to accept the imposed changes but incorporating them into existing modes of working, so that existing methods are adapted rather than changed and the effect of change is considerably different from that intended.

Creative mediation: taking active control of the changes and responding to them in a creative, but possibly selective way.

Retreatism: submission to the imposed changes without any change in professional ideology, leading to deep-seated feelings of resentment, demoralization and alienation.

Resistance: resistance to the imposed changes in the hope that the sanctions available to enforce them will not be sufficiently powerful to make this possible. (p. 36)

Supporting change in self and others

Most humans need to spend lengthy periods of time in supportive, collaborative groups if they are to learn effectively and be able to use what they learn. Teachers have known this about their pupils for years. What is not always acknowledged is that teachers in schools in this country are often isolated from each other for most of their working time. Elsewhere it is possible to find examples where two teachers work together full-time to share a class and teach in each other's presence, but the experience of many primary teachers in the UK is one of isolation from other adult professionals during the time when they are actively teaching.

Collaboration is vital for professional development but collaboration when actively teaching is not easy. It is more likely to occur away from the actual activity of teaching; over coffee and lunch breaks, at meetings, training days and school closures. For many teachers there are few opportunities to share teaching methods by actively teaching together.

It is worth bearing this absence of common experience in mind when thinking about the coordinator's response to those parts of the job description that ask for practical support for curriculum change and development.

A brief to carry out subject leadership and support curriculum change often anticipates the coordinator taking a leading role in:

- the introduction of new planning methods and formats;
- the introduction of whole school, year group or phase group planning to improve curriculum coverage, continuity and progression;
- the introduction of new teaching methods, including increased practical work, working on investigations, problem solving, discussion-based teaching, extended writing techniques;
- changes in the way the school's commercially produced schemes are used;
- developing the use of informal and formal observation of children at work as part of teachers' assessment;
- developing more effective ways of using practical equipment and resources such as Cuisenaire rods, base ten material, pattern blocks and calculators;
- the adoption and development of pupil self-assessment.

Clearly, these expectations require a substantial level of background knowledge of the teaching styles of colleagues throughout the school.

Your own staff development is vital. It begins with the support, training and guidance that is provided by the head and SMT as part of the role of subject leader. It should be accompanied by appropriate financial reward and a job description that defines and makes possible the carrying out of the work. The appointment should be seen as a personal investment in you as coordinator and subject leader. Meeting your needs, so that you can develop specific expertise, expand your subject and pedagogical knowledge, are expensive but worthwhile investments that will move the school on in its continuing efforts to raise the quality of the education it offers.

It's not selfish to expect and encourage professional investment in your developing expertise. One of the significant differences between teaching and other professions is the extent to which teachers are put into new situations with minimal training. Promotion to headship is a prime example and only now is this situation slowly changing. Teachers get used to feeling unskilled and have been told for years that money which is spent on their training is money taken away from children's education. This professional blackmail has created a climate in which teachers hardly even expect to be trained for new responsibilities.

The severe lack of professional development opportunities compared to many non-teaching jobs and the climate that this lack of provision generates, tends to cultivate two deprofessionalising situations: a) guilt at taking resources away from others for your own development; b) acceptance that the teaching hierarchy is naturally paternalistic and we should be grateful for what is 'given'. Neither view is acceptable.

Running workshops and staff meetings

Staff meetings are not always set up appropriately for inservice. The worst scenario is probably a meeting after school which is partly run by the head or deputy with a long agenda which over-runs, leaving you to do in twenty minutes what you had planned would take an hour. Business meetings are very often passive affairs with people receiving information and discussing points before moving on to the next agenda item. A maths meeting needs to be lively if tired teachers are going to be actively involved. If you have not run inservice meetings before then there are some gentle **starting points** which you might consider.

- Arrange if possible to have a meeting entirely dedicated to maths.
- Have a definite focus, a start time and a finish time and keep to them.
  'We're not all here but I think we need to start so we can get away on time.'

'There's fifteen minutes left before the end. I want us to finish on time so let's stop now and look at where we've got to and see what needs to be left to another occasion.'

■ Don't run the meeting on your own if you don't want to. Start with a topic that you feel confident about leading. Consider bringing in a local advisory teacher to run the meeting with you. One way of preparing for this, is by tackling a classroom topic alongside the advisory teacher in your room some days before the meeting. Children's work resulting from this can then be prepared for use at the meeting. Children's work provides a focus for teachers and doesn't force you into a position where you have to talk at them for an hour. Looking at children's work generates debate and opens your classroom to observation from colleagues. The 'Prime File' published by Simon and Schuster (PrIME, 1992) contains a wealth of ideas for running mathematics inservice. The OFSTED booklets on exemplification of standards (SCAA, 1995) has examples of children's work that often provokes lively discussion and provides a good starting point for levelling work and establishing a 'Standards Bank' for staffroom reference.

Brainstormings and mind maps

One way of working with the whole staff is to use **brainstorming**. This is often helpful in creating an active, participatory working environment and is appropriate for a whole range of issues. Here's one suggestion for tackling the topic of 'practical work in the classroom'. The starting point needs to be — established at a previous meeting — that people will bring to *this* meeting one resource or a single piece of equipment that they have chosen and which they find really useful when doing practical work in the classroom. In addition, they should bring something that children have produced as a result of working with the chosen resource — and you may want to suggest they bring two examples, one that includes pencil and paper work and something else (like a painting, clay or music, 3D models, etc.).

Some points to bear in mind when planning to run a brainstorm session with colleagues:
■ Create a practical environment and make it clear you expect people to work by arranging to have everyone seated round a large table.

- Start on time, but make sure you enthusiastically welcome anyone who does come late.
- Avoid someone else using the time to give out notices or starting the session for you — make it *your* meeting and do it your way!
- Have blank pieces of paper, pens, highlighters and scissors, ready. Have one card with the phrase *practical work* written on it.
- Draw up a timetable and keep to it.
- The starting point for the session is for each person to say out loud a single word or a short phrase that encapsulates what they think is associated with good quality practical work in the classroom. They call out, find a blank card, write their word or phrase on it and put their finished card on the table for everyone to see. No challenges or interruptions at this point. If someone doesn't understand what's written on a card they can ask later. You can contribute as well but hold back initially so you don't end up taking over with everyone listening to you.
- There's often a lull or a long silence after a few minutes of calling out. It's a good idea to weather this by sitting still, looking relaxed and smiling at people. Often it's the important issues that come out into the open after two or three minutes of silence. Don't appear edgy. Colleagues will assume you're waiting for them to continue and will try to think of new things to say.
- After a renewed burst of activity and when the next long silence descends, you will probably have enough material to work on. Tell them you're moving onto the next stage and ask them to read out the cards that have been written. Anyone can read them out, and now is the time to ask the original writer for clarification if anything is unclear. Duplicates can be removed and then some organising can take place. You can either ask everyone to look for cards that seem to go together in some way: this allows categories to *emerge*. Alternatively you can use key statements from a recent inspection report that refer to resources, or general statements about the use of resources taken from the teacher's guide of your mathematics scheme. Yet another way is to provide the following categories on separate cards in a distinctive colour: **knowledge**, **concepts**, **skills**, **attitudes**. People then work together reading out cards and sorting them following the agreed procedure.
- Encourage discussion about where individual cards should go and try to resist suggesting reasons yourself until the discussion is well under way. What usually emerges from the discussion are the school's strengths and weaknesses in relation to the subject in hand.

- You could draw this activity to a close by asking people what single idea they will take away with them, or you could make a list of the school's strengths and weaknesses.
- The session could close by referring back to the categories generated earlier with each person taking their five minutes to introduce their resource and the child's work that they brought. If you have little time or a large staff then this is better done at a second session.

Working in classrooms

The role of the coordinator has developed significantly in recent years and is still subject to rapid change. As soon as the National Curriculum required long-term, medium-term and short-term planning to be reviewed, and for new assessment procedures to be put in place in schools, coordinators took on new and very demanding work. When it became clear that inspectors needed to talk to a specialist with a whole school perspective, it became obvious that coordinators would need to acquire first-hand knowledge of whole school, **planning**, **implementation** and **evaluation** of the curriculum. These developments are forcing schools to find creative solutions to questions like:

- How is it possible to gain whole school knowledge of the curriculum as a class-based teacher?
- How can the coordinator play an effective role after an inspection?
- How can a coordinator effectively monitor whether last year's decisions about the maths curriculum are being carried out now that maths no longer gets prime staff development time?
- How can a curriculum leader demonstrate their good practice to colleagues when they have full-time responsibility for a class?

Future questions about the coordinator's role will include how to support colleagues when the 'basic numeracy centres' begin to produce highly prescriptive arithmetic programmes for children that demand an increased slice of curriculum time. Do we cut down work on data handling, algebra and shape and space, or postpone the teaching of humanities until Key Stage 3?

Financial support and the budget

Some of the biggest decisions that schools have had to take recently have centred around the way the school budget is managed. Many established heads have long since delegated control of curriculum budgets to coordinators. For newly appointed heads it is important to maintain close budgetary control over any area of the curriculum that is unfamiliar to them, especially if this is a relatively high spending area as mathematics can be. For the coordinator, to be left uninvolved in the management of the budget for your subject can present problems as well as being a lack of opportunity to develop expertise. A serious complication arises in schools that have retained the old practice of giving a yearly amount to each class teacher to spend. This does not represent effective budgetary control if the amount is a large proportion of the global sum available for maths. The maths budget is often best administered by the coordinator — provided the following issues are also dealt with.

Coordinators need clear guidance about how to use the school's internal accounting procedures and how to work closely with the school bursar. The maths budget should:
■ be set in relation to the whole school's curriculum needs, agreed through the school development plan;
■ be set according to current needs and not exclusively on historical spending habits;
■ be determined partly from school development plans (where new developments should be costed), and partly from agreed and identified recurring costs.

Most schools will be able to identify at least a few weaknesses in terms of books, equipment and resources. An audit of the whole mathematics curriculum inevitably throws up more demand than can usually be met by current levels of finance. Whatever method the school has for identifying priorities (and increasingly people look to coordinators for guidance on this) the coordinator is the person best placed to see that spending matches agreed targets throughout the year, by being the person responsible for using the budget to close the gaps that have been identified.

When the coordinator has a positive role to play in influencing the purposes for which the maths budget can be used, it is possible to look not just at children's needs but at teachers' needs too. Building up a small but supportive staffroom library with at least one dictionary of mathematics is best overseen by the coordinator.

Making time for talking

In one particular school, the only way I could manage was to get to school very early and get my classroom prepared before 8.15 am without any interruption. From then until 8.45 am I was available to colleagues. That simply isn't a realistic option for a large proportion of the workforce and working a lot of unpaid overtime is often counter-productive in the long term.

The successful school is a self-supporting community. Making time for talking allows the coordinator to maximise collaboration and support for colleagues — the benefit is a sharing of ideas and a feeling of being valued in your working community. Where opportunities exist to talk, to share ideas and concerns, there is the best climate for confident exploration of risky topics. In some schools, it's just not done to admit that you have problems organising certain ways of working. Instead of being seen as an inevitable consequence of working in a highly complex and rapidly changing professional field, the admission of difficulties is associated immediately with your personal qualities. Such a destructive view of humans is not what schools or education should be about. Somehow, the ability to view the world positively needs to become uppermost and those with management responsibility have a crucial part to play. By finding time to talk positively to colleagues about work in mathematics the coordinator can make a small but positive contribution to the overall climate.

Coordinators often find themselves, or put themselves, under pressure to 'prove' they've been carrying out their role. One danger is to go for greater formality, like holding more meetings, when it might not be necessary. Meetings are only one of the strategies open to managers. They are neither essential nor necessarily effective. Before deciding to have a formal meeting ask yourself what alternatives might be more effective. Brief, informal contacts with colleagues over coffee or lunch are often extremely effective ways of maintaining effective communication. Even when chatting briefly to colleagues you are:

■ keeping in touch;
■ communicating new ideas;
■ getting agreement;
■ identifying misconceptions;
■ collecting and disseminating information.

You could try to see how useful informal contacts are, without over-formalising the situation too much, by keeping an exercise book with you for one week in the term. Make that week a high profile 'maths week' and go out of your way to jot down the time, date, the topic and the name of the people you talk to. Use it later on in the term to review what you have covered. Check to see:

■ who you talked to and who you didn't (school secretary, postal workers, delivery drivers, classroom helpers, cooks, parents, governors . . .);
■ what you tended to talk about (and whether another week would be very different);
■ what you wanted and needed to say and ask;
■ what colleagues wanted you to hear from them;
■ the extent to which it was a 'typical' week;
■ what useful things came out of it;
■ what the conversations have led to.

Apart from reminding you how much important business gets done this way, it also provides a useful resource. Spend one week each term keeping detailed notes if you can manage to, and in between times just make brief notes but jot them in the same book, starting each week on a new page. At the end of a year you will have a useful resource that shows the concerns for that year, your leadership role and your response style. You don't need to show it to a subject inspector during an inspection but it could be useful when you prepare to meet a subject inspector because it will remind you of your previous year's work and allow you to draw together examples of your day to day work in managing the maths curriculum. If you're going for promotion, there will be lots of practical examples for you to use in describing your management style.

Figure 8.3 gives a list of questions that are useful in a variety of situations, even helping you prepare for an inspection. (A useful book on the whole issue of inspection is the *TES Guide to Surviving School Inspection* by Bill Laar, 1997, himself a registered inspector.)

Working alongside colleagues

Times in the school day when you are free of class contact offer rich opportunities for support and exchange of ideas, albeit for a few minutes only, snatched over a cup of coffee. The coordinator can maximise what little time there is by applying some simple rules of **time management**:

- Make lists of things to do and tick them off when you do them.
- Try to distinguish between *urgent* and *important* — you may impress people by always responding to the urgent things but in the long run you won't impress if you never get round to doing the important things.
- Aim to handle most of the memos, notes and letters that come your way *once only* and decide your options quickly: skim and scan to decide how much time they deserve. Respond *now* if it's a minor point. Decide a time to deal with it later if it really is your responsibility and you're busy now. Pass it back or pass it on but *get rid of it immediately* if it doesn't concern you.
- Be open and available to colleagues but don't try to solve other peoples' problems for them at the drop of a hat — invite them to come to you at a time that suits you.
- Don't go looking to help other people carry out trivial tasks — let them get on with theirs while you get on with

Aspects of the coordinator's role	How well can you answer these questions
Planning and organising the curriculum	How is it planned? How is the school organised?
Assessment, recording and reporting	How is assessment of children's attainment carried out? Is there any base-line assessment of children on entry to the school: do parents contribute in anyway? What classroom observation is carried out by teachers? Does teacher assessment cover all Programmes of Study? Is it well co-ordinated throughout the school? Does it focus on achievement or just deal with task completion? Is it discussed with children? Is it used to help children set themselves targets? Is it used to help plan future work? Is record-keeping carried out consistently throughout the school? Does it focus on achievement or just deal with coverage? Is it as economical and effective as possible? Is it kept in a form that is easily communicated to others: e.g. parents, other teachers, other schools?
Curriculum content	How do you ensure appropriate coverage across classes and throughout the school? How do you ensure equality of access and opportunity for all children and all abilities? How do you monitor continuity and progression of the taught curriculum?
Teaching and non-teaching staff	How is teaching effectiveness monitored? How effectively do teachers deploy themselves, learning support staff and volunteers? How do teachers monitor the effectiveness of the support staff and volunteers who work in their classrooms? How do you meet colleagues' immediate needs for support and guidance? How are the professional development needs of teaching and non-teaching staff met?
Resources for learning and accommodation	Does the school have a resources policy? Does it cover issues like: provision, use, storage, accessibility, health and safety? Are quality and quantity of resources including IT adequate and appropriate? How are staff made aware of resources and their effective use? Is there an inventory of resources? Do budget arrangements help to avoid unnecessary duplication or purchase of resources that may be under-used? Are resources in classrooms appropriately located, well labelled and accessible? Are centrally located resources accessible and labelled?
Management	How does the school ensure that: ■ The policy is consistent with other policies and meets the school's broad aims? ■ The policy is put into practice consistently through the school? ■ The curriculum planning, teaching, and assessment are monitored? ■ Initiatives are evaluated? ■ The policy is reviewed regularly? ■ The scheme of work meets National Curriculum requirements? ■ The scheme provides coverage, and appropriate guidance and support for staff?
Equal Opportunities and SEN	Is the curriculum appropriately matched to the needs of all children so that everyone has the opportunity to make progress irrespective of their prior attainment? Is there any special provision or arrangement made? Are the special needs of the most able recognised and met?
Contacts	Are there any special contacts made with parents, other agencies, institutions or industry and commerce to promote the subject? How is effective contact maintained with other schools to ensure continuity of mathematical experience across phases?
Coordinator's role	Is there a negotiated written job description? How is mathematics co-ordinated throughout the school? How are budgets managed? How is time created for you to carry out the various aspects of your role across the school? How do you communicate with SMT, colleagues?

FIG 8.3
Reviewing your role as maths coordinator

yours. Arrange to meet at another time to work on something important together.

■ Try to fix a regular time when people can see you and make it clear that there are certain times when you would prefer to be left alone to prepare your own classroom and to do your own thing.

■ People often stop us in the corridor and ask, 'Can I see you for a few minutes?' Think about how much time you *can really* spare now, and then *tell them*. Pass the decision back to them by offering more time when it suits you. 'I can only give you two minutes now. If you need longer then we could meet at . . . .'

■ Don't feel mean about saying *no*, be available on your own terms at least some of the time.

Maintaining an effective working relationship with the senior management team

The role of the coordinator is expanding and developing within a changing national scene. The job is challenging and complex, and you won't be able to do all the things that need doing. The crucial factor is whether the SMT **manages** the way you work by giving you clear goals and appropriate resources for you to carry out your job. Your responsibility is to carry out your job efficiently by, **prioritising** (including rescheduling and postponing), **managing your time effectively**, **delegating**, and **communicating effectively**. You will need to look to the senior management team for clear guidance, as well as carefully monitoring the way you manage your responsibilities. Some basic questions may help.

■ Is your work being effectively monitored by the SMT? Do you get help and advice about prioritising, etc. or are you being poorly managed by being left to struggle on your own?

■ Is your work sufficiently well defined by the SMT to maximise your chances of success?

■ Are you given the responsibility *and* appropriate resources (including time) by the SMT so that you have the wherewithal to carry out your duties?

■ Is your workload negotiated and regularly reviewed with the SMT to ensure you can realistically meet targets?

■ Are you actively supported by SMT and is your work monitored against targets which have been agreed?

■ Is there regular and effective two-way communication between you and the SMT with a readjustment of targets and workload in response to changing circumstance?

There is an important issue here about negotiating the tasks and the level of responsibility. Even in a small school of three or four teachers where everyone has several subjects to coordinate, it is unacceptably bad management to demand that everything asked for by SMT must automatically be carried out without discussion. It is a relic of the worst Victorian work ethic and has no place in the modern professional setting. There is a joint responsibility on the SMT and the coordinator to make the coordinator's role effective and manageable. SMT has to set clear goals and provide resources along with responsibility. Coordinators have to carry out their role effectively.

SMT and coordinators both have a responsibility to resist unrealistic demands and to ensure there are effective methods of negotiation in place within the school.

Reviewing practice

One of the most motivating ways of reviewing practice is to look at what children can do and what they produce. For the coordinator, a study of children's behaviour and activity should start with your own classroom practice and what your children produce. In the simplest of terms, we are looking for children who can demonstrate success:

■ by talking confidently and enthusiastically about their work;

■ by explaining what they've done;

■ by discussing and describing strategies they can use;

■ by demonstrating how they tackle mathematical tasks by showing how they use equipment, techniques and skills;

■ by finding ways of representing their results.

Immediate testing has some advantages but there is often even more value in seeing what children can do after a long break. At Helen's school, the autumn term started with a practical problem solving exercise in each of the subject areas. All the children in the school were set the same problem which was chosen to force them to draw on really secure, knowledge and skills established in their previous classes from before the long summer break. Helen reported that everyone, teachers and children, enjoyed starting the year by trying to solve practical and interesting problems. The range of solutions produced by the children clearly showed development and progression from Reception through to Year 6. Examples from the top, middle and bottom of each class were brought to a staff subject meeting and used as a basis for discussion about the quality of teaching and learning through the school. Teachers reported great pleasure and benefit in starting the year off in this way.

Part three | Whole school policies and schemes of work

Chapter 9
Recent changes

Chapter 10
A successful maths programme
for children

Chapter 11
Developments in curriculum
planning

Chapter 12
Developing a policy for
mathematics

Chapter 13
Long-term planning

Chapter 14
Medium-term planning

Chapter 15
Short-term planning

Chapter 16
Monitoring the planning

Chapter 9   Recent changes

Some of the recent changes can be illustrated through case study. At High Road primary, class teachers have between five and ten more children in their classes than five years ago. The way of working adopted by High Road is not intended as a rigid routine. Rather, teachers are encouraged to identify a small piece of work in maths to be taught directly and precisely, (e.g. teaching the idea that angle can be thought of as a measure of turn) and linking this to a larger mathematical topic on angles or a humanities topic on Great Explorers.

The long-term planning was agreed three years ago and follows a four year rolling programme. The long-term planning is a modified version of a bought, off-the-shelf package into which the school put its own favourite and already well-resourced topics — most of which are cross-curriculum rather than subject specific. The modified original sheets were photocopied and stored: the photocopies becoming the school's own definitive programme.

The long-term planning shows fortnightly topics on a term by term basis over four years, written in the minimum of detail, e.g. Shape in the Environment, Victorian Toys and Pastimes, Myself and Others. The teaching is planned to be taught in fortnightly blocks built around a single topic for the year group. For each topic teachers agree roughly how many lessons will be topic based and how many will be 'stand alone' maths lessons. The stand alone maths lessons relate closely to the topic but often teach specific skills and introduce new ideas that will be needed to support the skills and knowledge needed in the topic based maths work.

The medium-term planning was purchased as part of the same bought-in pack but needed very different adaptation before it became a suitable scheme of work. The original was produced on A3 sheets and an example is shown in Figure 9.1. A series of meetings continued for more than a year before a complete set of adapted sheets was produced. Less favoured activities described in the originals were blanked out. Teachers worked in year groups to trial and add their own activities.

There are many different types of medium-term planning being generated by schools and LEAs, many of which follow this type of format. To produce it all from scratch in a single school is a major undertaking and not necessarily the best use of time. The format has an impact on teaching style. The medium is the message, to borrow Marshall McLuan's phrase. The message being signalled here is — prepare and teach these practical activities with groups of children and use your published scheme pages to help consolidate the practical work.

Although very useful, there are disadvantages to the design. The original sheets were too crowded, especially at Key Stage 2, and as schools revised the contents the details had to be spread over many more sheets, involving much copying and pasting before a final version was completed and filed away. Most schools retained the original format and the sheets for mathematics appear in one of two styles. One type, following the example above, contains the whole of the mathematics curriculum presented entirely separately from the long-term topics and from the other subjects. This is a list of all the learning objectives organised by Programmes of Study and arranged in what is thought to be increasing difficulty. The other design is intended to strengthen cross-curriculum teaching. It has the topic title (taken from the long-term planning) at the top of the page followed by related learning objectives, including using and applying,

Mathematics
KS1
Stand Alone

SHAPE AND SPACE — PROPERTIES

Pupils should be given opportunities to: gain a wide range of practical experiences using a variety of materials, use IT devices, e.g. programmable toys, turtle graphics packages.

Pupils should be taught to: describe and discuss shapes and models, working with increased care and accuracy; begin to classify shapes according to mathematical criteria; recognise and use geometrical features of shapes, including vertices, sides/edges and surfaces, rectangles (including squares), circles, triangles, cubes, cuboids, progressing to hexagons, pentagons, cylinders and spheres; recognise reflective symmetry in simple cases.

LEARNING OBJECTIVES		SUGGESTED ACTIVITIES AND WAYS OF WORKING	RESOURCES
Pupils to be able to:	Using and applying		
describe and discuss shapes and patterns that can be seen or visualised;	Decisions (2a) Language (3a) Reasoning (4c)	Individual and group experiences with a wide variety of 3D shapes e.g. recycled box modelling, construction kit modelling. Give experience of handling cuboids, cubes, spheres, cylinders, cones.	Cardboard boxes of various shapes, Lego, Duplo,

FIG 9.1
A typical layout of a commercially produced planning sheet designed to become part of a scheme of work.

along with suggested activities and a list of resources. Suggested activities on the sheet relate to a range of different curriculum subjects and teachers use highlighter pens to identify the activities they have agreed to use in their year group planning meetings. Thus a topic of Victorians will have cross-curriculum work in maths that relates to Victorian toys and explores ideas in shape and space.

The school's adapted versions of the two types of planning sheets have been stored centrally and teachers take photocopies when they plan the next term's work. Space has been left on each page for teachers to add extra activities and further suggestions. They then plan a series of topics for the following term in fortnightly sequences.

Because the school favours a topic based approach, teachers tend to start their planning based on the list of topics fixed in the long-term planning. This shows them which medium-term sheets they need. They photocopy the relevant sheets and then use highlighter pens to indicate their choice of activities for coverage of the learning objectives. They then look at the maths knowledge and skills that are demanded by the cross-curriculum topics and use their analysis to guide them through the second (maths-only medium-term sheets) to identify key ideas that need to be developed to support the topic based work.

Teachers plan in year groups and the coordinator joins some of the planning meetings to give advice and monitor the procedure to see how effective it is turning out to be in practice. She also keeps a copy of each year group's highlighted planning sheets and stores them in the staff room for future reference and to monitor whether the intended continuity and progression throughout the school is achieved. As the year progresses the teachers can see from their highlighting what coverage of the curriculum they have achieved.

The design of the teachers' short-term planning is entirely their own choosing but has to show the fortnightly topic broken down on two sheets of a week each. This is where the teachers identify specific groups of named children, where they determine the timing, make notes about resources and identify pupils they will target for observation. The short-term sheets also identify the person who will support the children — the class teacher and/or the learning support assistant where there is one.

Increasingly, the coordinator has observed that the teachers at High Road plan a specific focus to their lessons. There is more practical work taking place and more mathematical discussion. Teachers are frequently starting lessons with an introductory whole class discussion followed by practical work and then a summary period where children talk together about what they've done.

Mathematics lessons are more often planned to be about something specific and a higher proportion of cross-curriculum topic work involves maths. Teachers have reported being able to keep children's interest going in maths for longer periods. It has been possible to make each lesson part of a series where the children follow an idea through in different ways, e.g. recognising shapes in their immediate environment; naming and describing properties of shapes; selecting material and resources that are most appropriate for the construction of their chosen 3D shapes; finding nets for the shapes; building homes for real or imaginary creatures; designing and making a building that has windows and doorways that are squares, rectangles, hexagons etc.

The coordinator and the staff reorganised their stock of commercially produced workbooks and worksheets so that relevant pages have been identified for each topic and entered onto the medium-term planning sheets. Teachers are moving towards using commercial materials near the end of each topic as a means of recording what children can do.

On three Friday afternoons each term the hall is turned over to the playing of maths games and activities to which parents are invited. Parents and children play games together for half an hour before the end of school. The coordinator has used this opportunity to encourage the playing of traditional board games at home and to demonstrate to parents the value of playing games in the learning of maths.

In summary, the coordinator feels that more teachers are providing a differentiated curriculum based on what they judge to be the range of abilities within the teaching group. Tasks are more often selected for groups of children on the basis of the children's recent and current achievement rather than groups being formed on age or friendship criteria.

In many schools, differentiation is being organised around setting. Children in several mixed ability classes are regrouped by ability following some form of assessment. In some schools this has become the way the entire maths curriculum is taught. In most schools setting is carried out for only some of the mathematics lessons: typically for three out of five of the children's mathematics lessons each week. Where a single class remains intact, the teacher is more likely than was the case three or four years ago to have all the children doing maths at the same time.

The changes have been wrought at some cost. Countless hours of work have been undertaken in thousands of schools. Some of the planning is still inefficient because it requires teachers to copy out large amounts of information unnecessarily. Some of the advantages are also obvious. A change to teaching a single topic over a period of time has allowed teachers to go into greater depth and detail in their teaching. Once the medium-term planning is in place in the amount of detail described above, it can become the school's scheme of work for mathematics. It contains not only the mathematics to be taught but also identifies the styles of teaching and learning that the teaching team subscribes to.

An effective scheme supports a greater choice of activities for teachers and clearer guidance on how to tackle a mathematical topic in a variety of ways. Activities for children can be selected to provide for a range of situations where:
- different types of resource can be used to tackle one problem in different ways;
- the same resource can be used in very different ways to tackle different problems;
- the teacher can switch between individual, group and whole class work as it seems appropriate within a single session;

- children of different abilities can all be made to feel they are contributing to the same topic;
- teacher assessment can include planned observation of groups of children on a more regular basis.

Teachers are more easily able to give children the direct input they need in order to understand mathematical concepts and to acquire appropriate skills and knowledge. Perhaps the single most crucial development in High Road primary and elsewhere is the increase in genuine discussion that teachers are able to organise with the whole class and with small groups.

Look at Figure 9.2 from your perspective as coordinator and use it to record your thoughts.

Ideas being explored with colleagues	Outcomes	Reasons for the outcomes
Starting lessons with direct teaching to the whole class.		
Increasing the quality and quantity of practical work for groups and individuals, including: games, puzzles, structured play, songs, rhymes, stories, etc.		
Planning consolidation and extension work so as to keep the whole class involved in the same topic.		
Increasing the amount of discussion and explanation in both whole class and small group situations.		
Increasing the number of investigations and problem solving sessions.		
Seeing textbooks, workcards and worksheets more as a means of consolidation and practise to be used towards the end of a topic, rather than as a teaching medium.		
Identifying small groups of children for observation and assessment for brief periods during some lessons.		

FIG 9.2

Putting ideas into context for mathematics coordinations

Chapter 10

A successful maths programme for children

For me the purpose of schooling is to allow children to demonstrate success, and to take learners to places where they are unlikely to travel alone. Many schools are successful in providing children with these opportunities but they have to work against a long-lasting Anglo-Saxon obsession. Historically, British culture and the British education system has always been obsessed with ranking children in order to identify those who have failed in some way. There is a deep-rooted cultural desire to see some children as successful and the rest as unsuccessful. Some years ago, children were ranked by 'intelligence' tests based on spurious scientific claims. Today, they are ranked by 'levels': the obsession continues. The ranking of children by levels offers them no better education today than ranking them by intelligence did in the 1940s and 1950s. It is the **teaching** and not the assessment system that raises standards of performance, understanding and motivation. Being given a performance ranking against one's peers is always based on partial information, never takes future performance into account, discourages motivation, and reduces emotional and intellectual resilience in many children. Let me be clear, evaluation of the teaching and learning process is essential, but the public ranking of children is an educational embarrassment.

The result of a *useful* education is that we develop a personal aptitude to tackle unknown, unforeseen and difficult problems in life. This requires a degree of confidence and access to a wide range of skills and knowledge along with the ability to call them up in new situations. In many ways the young baby's exploration of the immediate environment is a good model. A baby who is learning to stand may get frustrated when falling over but doesn't see falling as a failure. Babies make good use of everything they already know, using all the senses. We could do well to return to our earliest methods of problem solving and repeat the modes of learning we used as babies when we learned how to walk and to be more mobile and to speak our first language. As adults there is one further dimension to be added and that relates to our social awareness. As successful adults, and especially as teachers, we need to be sufficiently socially aware to be able to create a supportive learning environment for ourselves and for others.

A rationale for a mathematics curriculum

What should a mathematics curriculum for children try to achieve? The above philosophy requires that children are given opportunities to:

■ receive active teaching;
■ commit knowledge to memory;
■ have ideas explained to them;
■ apply basic skills of mathematics to a range of problems;
■ receive regular weekly if not daily practise of basic skills, techniques and strategies;
■ be actively involved in discussing and describing what they are doing;
■ be challenged to choose their own strategies and techniques when tackling problems;
■ work in an environment which supports their particular learning styles;
■ be exposed to ways of working that are unfamiliar and difficult;
■ work in an environment where it's OK to make mistakes;
■ find out when they have made mistakes, and to be encouraged to use their mistakes to re-think and re-explore their ideas;

- view difficulties encountered when solving a problem as an invitation to rethink the problem and continue the challenge; not as a way of being devalued as a person;
- explore pattern, logical reasoning and the internal structure of maths for its own sake, whether or not there is a practical, useful outcome;
- to work with mathematics that has practical applications that directly relate to their other interests.

A healthy exploration of mathematics encourages children to develop as healthy mathematicians. They have recall of basic facts, can use basic skills and techniques, can invent their own ways of tackling problems, and regularly (like all professional, adult mathematicians) spend a lot of their time being stuck on a problem. With help, discussion and collaboration, (again like professional, adult mathematicians) they can often see some different ways of trying to become unstuck. Above all, they see being stuck as a further, enjoyable challenge — not as a failure to be good at mathematics. Being a good mathematician involves working in all areas of maths. It is vital that children's mathematical experiences from pre-school onwards are broad and rich. We need numerate pupils but this does not mean focusing on number. Rather, being numerate is about ways of *using and applying* knowledge in all areas, including shape and space.

What does being numerate entail?

First and foremost, the numerate pupil is a **resilient** and **robust** learner, who can work with some measure of independence from the teacher and from friends. If we can establish classrooms which reflect most of the features listed above, we have created the right conditions for children to become numerate. A useful guide to numeracy in relation to number work and to the National Numeracy Project appeared in the magazine, *Primary Maths and Science*, (September 1997).

Being numerate includes:
1 Having the interest and motivation to take up mathematical challenges in all areas of the mathematics curriculum.

2 Being able to apply your knowledge
   situations relating to shape, algebra, n
   and to know what units of measurement a.
3 Being familiar with making and interpreting.
   charts; and graphs.

It is important that we use a broad definition of nume
that builds on current good practice. A broad definitio:
numeracy requires that children:

- have a sense of the *size* of the numbers they are working
  with;
- know where numbers fit in relation to a number line or
  number square;
- know their number bonds and tables by heart;
- can use: doubling; halving; rounding up and down;
  estimating and approximating; as strategies for carrying
  out calculations;
- can use what they know to attack all calculations
  mentally in the first instance;
- can use their initiative to modify problems, e.g. by
  choosing to count on, in order to solve a take-away
  problem;
- can calculate accurately, using their own chosen
  combination of mental, written and calculator strategies;
- can recognise when it is appropriate to use a calculator
  and do so competently;
- are able to read, interpret and discuss number problems
  presented in a variety of written styles;
- can match number problems to the appropriate operations
  needed to solve them;
- have ways of determining a reasonable answer at the
  outset, and have strategies for checking their answers for
  reasonableness;
- are able to use appropriate mathematical language to
  explain their reasoning and their methods.

How can maths lessons produce numerate children?

In the *Abacus*, Teachers' Books, (Merttens et al., 1997) there
is a theoretical model for the teaching and learning of

mathematics. It includes three elements or stages: **active teaching**; **making sense**; and **practice**. In some ways, this model of teaching can be applied to the lesson design that appears in the framework produced by the writers of the National Numeracy Project. The typical NNP lesson consists of about 50–60 minutes of oral and written work with an emphasis on: mental calculation; active teaching, making sense; and consolidating what you learn through practise. In the first 10 minutes, the teacher often works with the whole class to establish the focus of the lesson and to demonstrate the necessary skills. The middle part of the lesson involves the children working individually and in groups, making sense of the teacher's introduction by tackling related problems with practical equipment and resources. The final 10 minutes is often a whole-class, plenary session, where pupils: present their own findings; explain their work; sort out misunderstandings; reflect on the lesson; and on what needs to be remembered for the next lesson.

Children need lessons to be about something. They deserve to be told two things at the outset of every lesson, one is the purpose or focus of the lesson and the second is how **they** can judge for themselves that they've been successful during the lesson. This is best communicated at the outset by the teacher who says something along the lines of: 'This lesson is about. . . . You'll know if you've done well because you will be better at doing x.' At the end of the lesson, the teacher can remind the children of what was said at the outset and can choose a few children to demonstrate that they have developed further knowledge and skills. As a result of this regular communication about the purpose (as opposed to just communicating the content), children are better placed to make connections between things they've previously learned and what they are currently engaged on. A positive sense of achievement is being regularly reinforced but not in a trite way. Good use can be made of 'Smiley' stickers if children are able to select their own in order to signal their judgment of their own performance. Each child has an entirely free choice about the selection. They choose:

- a smiling face if they feel confident that they have understood the work completely;

- a straight face if they feel they have got the work right but don't really understand or think they will probably not be able to do the work in future;
- a sad face if they have struggled with the work and feel confused or frustrated.

Lessons should not all be the same — it's good to start a lesson with a puzzling situation, a mystery, a challenge — but children do best when they know explicitly how to assess for themselves whether they have been successful in achieving what was expected.

By contrast, children do not need a diet of lessons that are about being 'behind'. If one's mathematical experience consists of being told one needs to 'catch up' either with 'the clever ones' or with some externally imposed programme that requires a certain speed, then this — and not the mathematics — is what will be remembered. The classroom where some children are always one work book 'behind' the others is not an stimulating place to be or a place where effective learning is going to occur.

Key features in successful mathematics teaching

Recent research (e.g. Reynolds and Farrell, 1996) suggests that British children are less able than children in some other countries to use mathematics to tackle problems. A 'traditional' versus 'progressive' argument has erupted but in my view this is inappropriate in the context of a professional debate, only benefiting those with a political axe to grind. Such either-or drum beating hides too many of the fundamental issues. The research sought to get children to apply their mathematical knowledge and many were unable to do this.

Throughout the country there are teachers who use a wide range of teaching styles. Some have a predominant style but many others are eclectic in their choice. It is unlikely that any one teaching style can cause such a broad deficit. What is more likely is that there are weaknesses contained within many of the teaching styles used.

Fundamental to effective teaching and learning of mathematics is a cycle of active teaching or exposition, practise, practical exploration, investigation and problem solving. These activities are all carried out within a classroom environment that encourages wide-ranging discussion. Despite the recommendations of the Cockcroft Report some sixteen years ago (see para. 243 for a list of opportunities children should have in their maths curriculum), there is little evidence of the elements of this cycle being systematically carried out in more than a small minority of classrooms. The predominant style (and one which in my view has contributed more powerfully to children's lack of understanding and competence in maths) is the use of textbooks, workbooks and worksheets, **as the main or sole medium for delivering the curriculum to children.**

Using commercial maths schemes

Commercial mathematics schemes fall into three broad types:
1 Textbooks, consumable workbooks and a limited form of teacher's guide. The original versions often pre-date the National Curriculum and have been modified to conform to current demands. Frequently mathematical topics are scattered throughout the pages in a random fashion, designed to alleviate boredom rather than fit together in a coherent whole. It is difficult to see what the children's yearly diet is going to be in each area of maths without chopping up a pupil's workbook and gathering together the pages that relate to each topic.
   The assumption that a commercially produced scheme meets the requirements of the National Curriculum is based on the idea that the National Curriculum is solely related to content. Apart from the danger of gaps (insufficient data handling or algebra) and over-emphasis on certain aspects of number (too much undifferentiated written computation), the whole issue of *using and applying* is seldom addressed appropriately. Partly because of insufficient opportunity to explore mathematics practically through investigations and problem solving, and partly because of the teaching styles that are often provoked by textbook and workbook focused learning,

there is a grave danger of children not being able to recall the mathematics they are taught **and** not being able to apply what they can recall.

2   More recent schemes like that produced by Nelson Publishers, (*Nelson Mathematics*) have a desk top file as a central resource which contains highly detailed teacher's notes. The work is often broken down into mathematical topics and the topics can be arranged in the order chosen by the teacher. There is often a useful balance between exposition and practical activities designed to reinforce the ideas introduced by exposition. As these schemes have been adopted so the number of schools reporting difficulties has increased. Again, the nature of the workbooks and the pressure produced by sheer mass of content, together with the dominant teaching style of some teachers has led to the teachers' files being under-used and the mathematical diet of the children reduced to colouring in the workbooks.

3   A very small clutch of schemes, of which *HBJ Mathematics* (Harcourt Brace Jovanovich) is a useful example, set out to organise children's mathematical experience around themes, some of which naturally extend to a variety of other curriculum areas whilst others are chosen for the opportunities to provide for in-depth study of mathematical topics in their own right. Topic-based schemes can work well in single-age classes but present organisational difficulties when children are taught in classes spanning two or three year groups (which is often the case in small schools). They also tend not to provide sufficient structured practice at computation. Where the teacher and the children find the topic sufficiently challenging these schemes are very effective and often give sound advice about developing opportunities for children to work on the learning objectives set out in the *using and applying* PoS. However, teachers face difficult problems over planning when children find the topic difficult and need more time than has been allocated if they are to assimilate the work in the current topic.

The most damaging schemes are those that attempt to provide 'individualised' learning. It is not always the intention of authors and publishers to provide 'individualised' materials. Teachers in some schools have simply let children work through pages at their own speed. This way of working can have disastrous results on children's levels of understanding, and particularly on their ability to discuss and explain what they are doing. One effect of individualised programmes has been to reduce the range of teaching styles available to classroom teachers. More than any other single factor, individualised programmes have led to severely limited opportunities for interactive teaching — what Cockcroft called 'exposition'. Textbook and workbook materials are most effective when they are used to provide practice and consolidation **after a period of active teaching or exposition**. In practice more often than by design, textbook, workbook and worksheet schemes have rendered an active teaching approach to mathematics almost impossible to initiate. Where these schemes are over-influential in dictating the predominant style of teaching and learning the consequences are:

- Children are expected to learn their maths from a series of pages — a largely ineffective process which disrupts the development of reasoning, argument and proof (thinking processes that require a considerable verbal component in both children and adults and which are suppressed).
- Children are often working on different pages with widely differing content, rendering active teaching to a group virtually impossible.
- The teacher's role consists not so much of creating conditions for mathematical talk but in providing technical instructions about how to tackle the pages, what the author really meant, which bits to colour in, which bits to leave out, how many pages to do today, and so on.
- Discussion between pupils and with the teacher is extremely difficult because there is no mathematical focus to lessons, children are tackling too many different areas of mathematics.

The absence of discussion is disastrous. Discussion is very effective in helping teachers to identify what children know with confidence and what has only partially been grasped. If there is a focus to the lesson, the teacher has a genuine choice about how to proceed. Whole class, small group and individual work are all possible and at different times they are all appropriate. To follow a period of active teaching or exposition (which could be as short as ten minutes or as long as an hour) children will need time on their own to practise, time with peers to extend the new ideas and skills into new areas and time to consolidate and demonstrate what they can do. It is at this stage that textbook, workbook and worksheet schemes have their usefulness. The teacher can invite children to demonstrate through the pages of the scheme what they already know and can do. This period of repetition and revision is useful if newly learned skills and ideas are to become secure.

Using computers

Many teachers find computers are not easy to incorporate into mathematics teaching. There are many skills to be learned by children. Close supervision and guidance, if only for brief periods of time, are essential if children are to learn efficiently, and many teachers find the provision of this close teaching very difficult to arrange. Software has to be appropriate for the children and this has been surprisingly more difficult to achieve in maths than might have been anticipated. As ever there's still a lot of poor quality software around, some of it on CD ROM. There was a lot of useful software for the old BBC and RM machines and just because it's old doesn't mean it hasn't got a use. My own view is that the most recent and technologically advanced hardware should go to the youngest children because as hardware and software designs have improved the whole process of using the computer has been simplified. A 4 year old can more easily manage a CD ROM than a BBC B and a 10 year old can manage a BBC B perfectly well. Whoever gets the newest hardware, the main issues are:

- the quality of software available;
- clear planning that identifies why the computer is being used for this task at this time;
- what level of expertise is expected of the children and how they are expected to acquire it;

- ensuring that there are opportunities for discussion and for extended periods of work on the computer;
- ensuring that any supporting adults have a sufficiently high level of expertise;
- knowing how much actual mathematical thinking is being developed as children work on the computer.

Many schools have found creative solutions to some of these problems. In one school, a retired teacher who wanted to spend a few fours a week with children offered her services free and worked with every single child in Key Stage 1 in a very supportive way, using the school's IT software map and ensuring basic skills were in place. Even many of the youngest children were virtually self sufficient in finding and loading software and use of the mouse. This freed the teachers to teach the curriculum. Another infant school decided to dedicate a room to IT. This meant it could be timetabled and the timetable was public. From minimal use the teachers moved very quickly to high levels of use because the timetabled sessions meant planning to use the room. The coordinators had ensured the production of a manageable software map for IT that effectively supported work in the other subjects. Together they gradually built up a list of activities in each curriculum area. The maths activities were then incorporated into the medium-term planning/scheme of work and supported the maths curriculum well.

Many teachers feel that IT comes a long way down their list of things to tackle when faced with implementing the maths curriculum. Trying to do too much often results in achieving very little and feeling frustrated. It's better for teachers to make a resolution that they can keep; for example, to learn to use *one* new piece of software each year. As a coordinator, you need to temper enthusiasm for the good use of computers, with a realisation that teachers have a right to have time for learning. Focusing on one piece of software for a year group is better for many teachers than the invitation to choose from half a dozen bits of software. The use of a small set of carefully chosen software is much more likely to lead to high quality use of computers for teaching mathematics.

Using calculators

The use of calculators has seldom been far from the headlines. The range of views expressed in the press and elsewhere demonstrate that the effective use of calculators is not a simple business. I would suggest that the teacher's primary objective is to create robust learners, i.e. children who enjoy struggling with mathematical problems, even when they get stuck. Producing a class full to robust or resilient learners requires that they have plenty of factual knowledge and that they understand some big ideas. They need to have more than just a set of skills. They also need the ability to call on their skills, build them into strategies at will and know that they have permission to invent their own ways of doing things.

In your whole school role, do you know the range of experiences available to children throughout the school? Have you discussed your views about calculators with your colleagues? You may need to take a lead on this issue because many people both inside and outside schools have firm but naïve views about calculator use. If you haven't got a school policy on the use of calculators you should consider developing one, but without rushing into a dogmatic statement. It's a complex issue that goes right to the heart of effective teaching and effective learning. It may be that you need to sit on the fence for a while and mull things over.

One useful way of proceeding is to treat calculators like any other ordinary piece of equipment for a while and then review progress. Another way is to restrict children's access to them for a while by limiting calculator use to one lesson a week. After a term, you can review what you have learned about the benefits and limitations of using and not using them. Drawing up a table of advantages and disadvantages based on your own immediate experiences can be a helpful place to start shaping a policy.

Teaching the skilful use of calculators can lead to big developments in children's mathematical understanding. These developments are well documented, for example, in the report on CAN (1991) (Calculator Aware Number

Curriculum). The CAN Project which was part of the PrIME project, found evidence that children could develop a sound understanding of number through work that incorporated a high level of calculator use.

A careful balance needs to be struck between standard procedures and children's own methods. Both are acceptable and appropriate. Sometimes, however, standard methods are unnecessarily formal and cumbersome because they originated as written methods used by accountants in Victorian times and were designed primarily to allow visual checking of financial and business transactions in ledgers. Children's invented methods are not always efficient and they need to be encouraged to modify them to improve their efficiency and the speed of calculation.

Teachers need to monitor children's choices and to guide them to improve the quality of their decision-making; for example by taking a short lesson, once a week — every week — for ten minutes, exploring just one calculation in depth. Choose a calculation that is within the children's capability, and look at how it would be performed when: tackled mentally; with a calculator; using pencil and paper. These short lessons can gradually develop so as explore situations where part of a calculation may require mental computation and another part may require another method. Taking the time to look at one calculation in depth and providing them with the answer at the outset, frees children from having to focus on getting a correct result and emphasises your intention to focus on the *processes* involved in moving between the three methods.

What's involved and what's assumed in teaching for understanding?

'Teaching for understanding' is a phrase heavy with implication and is not always to be read literally. Looking at an example of some teaching might be a helpful way in which to open out the discussion. Conventional wisdom suggests, for example, that children need to understand place value if they are to successfully perform written methods of subtraction based on decomposition, otherwise they 'won't know what they are doing'. Here, teaching for understanding has led us astray. The traditional methods of written computation were designed to make the working transparent (so, for example, that financial accounts could be checked). They were not developed to be useful teaching and learning aids and they are neither easy to learn nor are they essential. Our argument about teaching for understanding obliges us to teach how place value works and why standard written algorithms, like the decomposition methods of subtraction, function as they do. It took the western world until about AD 800 to accept the current place value system and yet we expect 7 year olds to master it. Our initial intention to get children to do addition and subtraction calculations on paper has been subverted by pressure to *always* teach for understanding. Isn't there a more effective method of teaching written computation methods that avoids the premature demand for a full explanation of place value?

In my opinion, what is needed is much more time spent on mental computation work and less in the early years on written computation. Let's suppose that mental work takes place as part of almost every lesson and that our main intention is to ensure almost everyone acquires a fairly swift and accurate recall of all number facts to 10 at least during Year 1 and at least to 100 by the end of Year 2. This would require the teaching of strategies and techniques including extensive use of finger counting, committing number facts to memory, extensive work with the decades and, most significantly, much more work with number lines and less time spent on cardinal counting of objects. Taking away would now be now taught primarily as counting on, an efficient method of finding the difference between two numbers on a number line, first by touching the number line and physically counting the jumps from one number to the next, later by looking at the number line and mentally calculating, and finally calculating mentally with no number line visible (but hopefully an internalised mental image of one available).

Our expectations for children in this situation would be that all work is done mentally well before pencil and paper methods are introduced. What do we learn from a study of mental calculation strategies? They are often adjusted by the person doing the calculation. For example, the teacher asks how would you work out 81 take away 14? One child answers, I think of 80 take away 10 take away 4 and put 1 back. Another says, I go up from 14 to 20 then go up in tens to 80 and then on 1 more. What distinguishes these methods from traditional written methods? Mental methods often start by adjusting the sum to get a more convenient equivalent. This is often followed by dealing first with the digits of highest value, in this example the tens. Counting on is often chosen in preference to counting back or taking away.

Now, after all this mental computation, we want to introduce some written methods — but it will be to children who have experienced hours of mental computation until they are fluent and confident. Why use the traditional methods? These addition and subtraction routines require starting with the units. There are other methods around. Methods that replicate on paper what children have learned to do in their heads and which are therefore more likely to strengthen the mental methods built up over a long period.

Spending considerably more time on mental work may be rejected because it demands different rituals than those that young children are currently introduced to, when they first come to school. To some teachers the activities suggested here feel like rote learning — like learning *without* understanding. Suppose for a moment we shift our attention from what we have traditionally sought as evidence of understanding and refocus on some other skills and knowledge. We shift from learning to perform traditional computation to learning to carry out most calculations mentally. We shift our emphasis from an ability to count sets of objects in order to perform a calculation like 22 add 7, to an ability to 'read' a number line. We emphasise an ability to recall complements to 10, to 20 and further — (to know that 6 and 4 are complements to 10; 16 and 4 are complements to 20).

Let me be very clear, it is not my suggestion that teaching should not lead to understanding — of course it should.

Rather, I am arguing that a belief that understanding should **always accompany** a period of learning not only leads us to some odd and unrealistic expectations, but also can, in some circumstances, put unnecessary pressure on children to perform. The ability to perform most calculations mentally could lead to significant improvements in children's ability to approximate, estimate, round numbers up and down and convert calculations into more convenient equivalents. Pencil and paper routines that follow similar procedures to children's mental methods are more likely to be retained and errors more easily detected. It is this approach, rather than arguments about teaching styles that will lead to improvements in children's performance in arithmetic.

Chapter 11 — Developments in curriculum planning

The three most influential pressures on curriculum planning are:
- changes to the way in which schools carry out assessment recording and reporting of children's achievement;
- preparation for and response to the school inspection programme;
- changes to the structure and content of the National Curriculum.

In many schools, planning has been substantially developed over recent years. The most notable achievements have been:
- a questioning of the way mathematics relates to the rest of the school curriculum;
- a much clearer picture of the maths curriculum throughout the school;
- more clearly delineated responsibility for content in each teaching group;
- more consistent planning of maths lessons within the school;
- an improvement in the quality of investigations and problem solving;
- an increase in practical work in response to the *using and applying* PoS statements;
- a harmonising of marking policy and assessment and record-keeping procedures throughout the school.

This is an immense amount to achieve in a short space of time and has been achieved through careful planning. There is considerable variation between planning documents in different schools and this is evidence that there is no single right answer: planning must match the needs of the individual school and its pupils. One particular area of concern that teachers regularly report on courses is difficulty in the production of medium-term plans. Many teachers say that the methods they are using require them to write out the same information several times in different formats: a practice that is inefficient and wasteful of their time. An important role of the coordinator can be to undertake the review of planning procedures and make suggestions that reduce the workload whilst still providing the information that is needed. Improving the efficiency of the planning process is not a trivial matter, however, and over the next few chapters we will be looking in detail at the planning process.

In summary, good planning:

- clearly communicates to both experienced and inexperienced teachers exactly what is to be taught, and provides choice rather than becoming dictatorial and over prescriptive;
- provides a clear map of the mathematics curriculum to parents;
- provides a choice of activities, resources and ways of working that opens up new ways of teaching;
- allows full coverage of the school's mathematics curriculum, both the legally required National Curriculum and those activities the teachers have decided to provide in addition;
- ensures resources are used to maximum effect. This includes guidance on deploying human resources to ensure, for example, effective support of children with special needs;
- ensures children meet the mathematics they need and can cope with so they can demonstrate success;
- ensures equality of access and opportunity, parity of work between parallel classes and continuity and progression throughout the school;
- maximises opportunities for teachers to plan with creativity and invention while minimising the time and effort needed to carry out the formal writing of the planning documents themselves;
- makes clear the links between maths and other curriculum areas and maximises the teachers' opportunities to develop those links soundly;
- helps teachers to select and devise activities which most closely match the needs of children in their class in relation to the range of abilities and interests;
- provides a choice of routes through the curriculum so that children are not faced with a single, continuous, identical diet;
- provides guidance and suggestions for assessment opportunities from the outset.

The elements of current planning

There is a need to show how the curriculum content that the school chooses to teach complies with national statutory requirements. This normally means ensuring that the planning shows how all the learning objectives required in each Key Stage receive appropriate attention: and in mathematics this is a major undertaking. Many schools have chosen to do this in what they call their medium-term planning documents. It is this planning that is the most complex, onerous and difficult to carry out, as it shows how learning objectives will be linked to classroom activities. Schools tend to diversify here. Schools that see published schemes as defining an appropriate curriculum and thus rely heavily on published scheme material for their teaching tend to identify parts of their chosen scheme resources as providing access to the learning objectives. My argument is that a curriculum should not be defined by a published scheme but must include the actual teaching behaviour or style of the teachers, along with opportunities for practical work and the proper development of the learning objectives related to *using and applying*. Schools that have taken an approach which is less dependent on published schemes tend to identify areas of mathematical **knowledge**, **concepts** and **skills** and match these to the learning objectives. This latter group of schools may also tend to provide more practical work for children since once the knowledge, concepts and skills are mapped against the learning objectives, a whole range of supporting activities and resources can be cross-referenced.

Many schools have opted to purchase a basic medium-term plan that provides activities mapped against learning objectives. Schools can then trial these materials and add their own references to schemes and resources for investigation and problem solving work. The purchasing of medium-term planning materials doesn't necessarily mean less work for teachers, but rather a different kind of work. Absorbing them into current practice can be complex and modification is essential. There are LEAs that provide and sell these materials (like Cornwall LEA) and the Cornwall

Planning Pack is a good example of the comprehensive response to schools' requests for support in developing whole school planning. It consists of detailed examples of a model of long-term planning using a rolling topic programme together with medium-term planning materials that can form the basis of a scheme of work for all subjects including mathematics. Maths topics and activities are shown linked to other subject areas on A3 sheets called Cross-curriculum Maths and a substantial set of sheets show maths activities in what they have called their Stand Alone Maths sheets — also A3 format. These latter cards show all the learning objectives for mathematics matched against activities, investigations and problems which are briefly outlined for the teacher. Various blank sheets suggest ways in which long-term, medium-term, and short-term planning can be recorded. The material is also sold as a set of computer disks as well as hard copy so that schools can more easily make the materials their own after trialling the basic version.

Still to be dealt with is the short-term planning of individual teachers. It is this level of planning that determines the pace and structure of each day or week. While the medium-term planning offers a choice of activities which help teachers teach and children work on a particular learning objective, the short-term planning identifies the actual grouping of children. In addition it will show exactly which activities have been chosen, and where the teacher has modified activities to meet the needs of children of different abilities. Resourcing requirements need to be pinpointed in this planning, together with the timing of the lessons, which have to fit within the weekly routine. Decisions also need to be made in advance about opportunities for informal and formal assessment.

Many teachers' short-term planning is idiosyncratic and emerges partly as a consequence of their own learning styles. Some people function best with lists, others prefer diagrams and need to start with a topic web for a week or fortnight and embellish it. Insistence on rigid conformity may easily lead to a prescribed layout that doesn't suit some people. It's

Things to consider:
- A weekly plan can provide evidence of continuity and progression in a way that a series of daily plans may not do so easily.
- Daily plans allow more space to write and most people will need an A3 sheet to show a weekly plan.
- If you have very large writing, or you use drawings containing clusters of ideas connected by arrows, then a weekly sheet probably won't be sufficient on its own.
- Incorporating a space for informal observation of a selected group of children may simplify the monitoring process and cut down on the number of pieces of paper needed.
- A supply teacher needs to be able to make sense of the short-term plans as they stand.
- An inspector will need to see a daily plan with timings during an inspection — whatever else you normally do.

worth encouraging colleagues to talk about their short-term planning because:
- it's often very creative;
- very flexible;
- allows for changes to routine with minimum disruption;
- is a fundamental source of confidence because it allows teachers to know exactly what they have to do next and what each child or group is required to do;
- it often gets modified as it is used and the reasons for modification are a valuable talking point.

It is also useful to review individual short-term planning together and to identify key basic ground rules within which teachers feel they can operate.

Chapter 12   Developing a policy for mathematics

The Oxford dictionary definition includes references to
insight, *practical wisdom*, and *following a course of action*.
In one sense no school can fail to have a mathematics
policy. The practice and the policy are both descriptions of
the mathematics that is taught in a school. Practice and
policy are inseparable. The difficulties that teachers faced in
the early years of the National Curriculum came partly from
having received little guidance about the form a written
policy should take. The emergence of a common approach to
policy documents has meant that things are now somewhat
easier. Policy statements should emerge from, and describe,
current practice. A written policy statement which does not
describe, reflect and guide current practice is not only
unhelpful but also potentially divisive. When a policy
document does not embrace current practice it can't easily
acknowledge current levels of practical wisdom nor can it
describe the current course of action that the staff are taking.
The most likely results are a document full of wishful
thinking, pious hope and a lack of connection with practice
that does not bear scrutiny. The major challenge is to
produce a written statement that:

- shows how the teaching of mathematics fits with the
  school's overall teaching intentions;
- states how the school's general aims are realised in the
  mathematics curriculum;
- realistically describes current practice;

- shows links with those aspects of the school development plan that demonstrate how the school team intend the current practice to develop;
- provides an appropriate introduction to the mathematics scheme of work;
- shows how the policy document for mathematics fits with other policies.

An important decision in planning a written policy statement is to consider postponing the writing of it. Consider, instead, meeting as a whole staff to discuss and agree a verbal description of current practice that can be used as a basis for a written description of 'the teaching that currently exists'. As this statement of current practice begins to take shape, match it to the school's general aims and ethos. Don't try to fudge things: point out where there are strong links and where gaps exist. For example, school brochures often claim to give children opportunities for independent thinking. Although this may be obvious in PE and games, art and music, children in some schools have little opportunity to choose what to do and how to do it within the school's maths curriculum. It's useful to ask where the school's aims for children are regularly provided for in the mathematics curriculum.

By all means review any policy documents already in existence. Spend time deciding how best to describe what happens when you currently teach mathematics. Only when the staff in a school have a common language in which to describe their current practice, can they begin to articulate the extent to which their beliefs and values are evident in the opportunities for mathematical thinking that are available to children. From here, it is possible to publicly celebrate what you are already doing well. You can identify the factors that are active in promoting good practice and communicate them to colleagues. Try to bring out into the open those factors that are limiting the quality of what is being offered to children.

Experienced and newly qualified teachers, together with learning support assistants and other adults who support classroom work, all need to have easy access to the language in which we describe, explain and comment on mathematics education for children. There needs to be a common understanding of practice and the language that is used to describe children's mathematical activity. When you talk about 'open-ended work', 'doing an investigation', do all the adults who support maths in the school understand and use the language in similar ways? Is there a clear understanding about how help is given to children who are 'stuck'. Is being 'stuck' seen as all right or as evidence of failure by some people?

If you work on common understanding and common forms of language, the unique nature of the school and what it offers is then more likely to emerge in a clear and easily understood way. The written statement of policy that you finally produce can be seen more clearly to reflect the values and beliefs prevailing in your school. Current practice can then be described in a much more informed and informing way.

Leading on from a common language of current practice, the future development of the mathematics curriculum is easier to write — though it may well end up being written later than you had originally intended. Statements of intent and planned developments will appear complete and realistic, fitting what everyone knows is the current scene. A written policy that is based on current practice is more likely to:

- be realistic;
- be coherent;
- be relevant;
- achieve any goals set;
- be acceptable to all parties involved;
- be a positive influence on the maths curriculum for children;
- be a positive stimulus to staff development.

It's easier if maths has been singled out for special treatment because this often means there is some staff development time set aside during meetings and training days for work with colleagues. There may be some money available from the staff development budget that can pay for a small amount of non-contact time. GEST funded courses give opportunities to meet colleagues from other schools, a chance to update subject knowledge and time for writing. If however, developing the maths curriculum is currently a low priority in the school, but requires a lot of work, then the task facing you is much more difficult and is likely to take a lot longer. It's possible that there is no maths policy or that existing documents are out of date because of recent changes, e.g. school amalgamation.

Getting started when there is no existing written policy

It cannot be emphasised too strongly that the writing of the school's policy should be the result of discussion and full collaboration with colleagues. Often, coordinators find that providing a semi-structured start makes things easier for colleagues to contribute. It's helpful to break down the policy into several sections. Where colleagues feel unable to contribute directly to the *whole* task, then the coordinator can organise small groups to take one or two sections each on which to work. It's not essential that everybody tackles every section, but make sure you include as many of the teaching and non-teaching staff as you can, and try to match the sections to colleagues' own interests. You can then combine their contributions into a draft document for everyone to examine later. You could do all of this in a workshop situation (see the section which follows on **running a workshop for developing a policy statement**). The following sections are the ones most schools include in their policy statements. There's no single correct format to a policy statement, and no perfect order to the sections. The objective should be to produce a document that accurately reflects the school's broad aims, describes the range of current practice, and signals the school's proposed developments in the mathematics curriculum.

Possible sections to be included in a policy document

1 **The nature of mathematics**
What do we mean when we think and talk about mathematics in the broadest sense? What is mathematics?

2 **How classrooms are set up for mathematics**
A broad, simple, jargon-free description of current classroom organisation, typical classroom routine and day-to-day management. How much time per week is typically available? What resources and equipment are used? How are children grouped? What opportunities are taken: to provide active teaching to the whole class and to small groups; to monitor groups at a distance; to provide individual work for children? How is children's progress monitored? How are children expected to record their findings? How are children gradually trained to select their own resources, their own mathematical problems, ways of working and ways of representing the results of their mathematical work?

3 **Children's mathematical experiences**
What do the children regularly have to do? What range of mathematical activities is commonly available? What is typically expected of them? What opportunities are there for: play; construction; using practical equipment to represent mathematical problems and situations in shape, space and measures; number; algebra; data handling? What opportunities are there for children to: work independently; discuss their ideas in peer groups; contribute to whole class lessons? What opportunities do children get to select their own resources, their own mathematical problems, ways of working and ways of representing their findings? What opportunities do they have to describe their work to their peers?
How much variation is there in children's experiences across age groups, ability groups and classes? How is continuity monitored between classes of similar age and ability? How is progression monitored across age and ability groups? What do base-line assessments show of the capability of the youngest children?

4 **Equality and justice**
What arrangements are made for monitoring equality of access and opportunity so that all children can engage in the whole mathematics curriculum, regardless of gender and culture? What opportunities are taken to identify, explore and celebrate mathematical ideas from different cultures? What opportunities are given to children (e.g. during circle time) to comment on their own progress, to show positive attitudes to

the subject and discuss the opportunities available to them in the mathematics curriculum?

5 **Special educational needs**

What arrangements are made for identifying, monitoring and supporting children with special needs? How do arrangements in mathematics meet school policy requirements and children's legal entitlement?

6 **Current practice, Desirable Outcomes and the National Curriculum**

How does current practice fulfil the requirements: across all areas of maths; across all parts of the Desirable Outcomes; across all NC Programmes of Study? How is access to the areas of Desirable Outcomes and the National Curriculum monitored? How is the use of commercial schemes managed so that these expectations and requirements can be met? How is the school's broad policy on assessment interpreted in the case of mathematics?

7 **Arrangements for ensuring the development of numeracy**

How is numeracy identified in the: planning; teaching; and assessment of mathematics?

How is the development of children's numeracy ensured in classroom teaching?

In relation to numeracy, how is teaching and learning monitored?

8 **Children's records of their work**

How are children generally expected to represent and record their findings? Do opportunities include written prose, diagrams, oral reports, the use of IT, painting, drawing, music, dance? How is evidence of children's progress with practical work represented and recorded? How is the marking of children's written work carried out and how does marking of work conform to the school's general policy? What work is retained and used to contribute to individual children's records of achievement and what criteria are used for selection?

9 **Cross-curriculum links**

What opportunities are taken to use mathematics in other areas of the curriculum? How and when are mathematical knowledge, skills and attitudes made use of within other curriculum contexts (e.g. through children's story books and story writing)?

10 **Assessment, recording and reporting**

How are teachers encouraged to monitor children's performance and make informal assessments? What type of 'pupil tracking' is used? How does informal and formal assessment in mathematics fit with the general school policy? How is the recording of children's achievement carried out and how does it meet the school's current policy and legal requirements? What arrangements have been made to provide staff with an effective 'standards bank' containing a range of 'levelled' work for reference and guidance?

11 **Staffing responsibilities and resources**

What is the current staffing for mathematics, including classroom support provided by learning support assistants, volunteers, parents and others? How are arrangements supervised and who is responsible for ensuring they are carried out appropriately? How do the arrangements for staffing of mathematics and classroom support comply with the school's general policy and with any regulations in force on adult access to children? What are the current arrangements and responsibilities for: managing the maths curriculum; the maintenance of resources and materials; the support available to colleagues (e.g. mentoring of newly qualified teaching staff, new learning support assistants)?

12 **Staff development and links to school development plan**

In broad terms, what initiatives are being undertaken to strengthen the mathematics curriculum? What outside agencies are regularly used? How is good practice communicated between colleagues and throughout the school? How is the coordinator enabled to support colleagues?

13 **Special links with outside bodies**

What special links does the school exploit in regard to mathematics with business, commerce, industry and farming, public agencies, museums, shops, etc.

14 **Curriculum evaluation**

What steps are taken to monitor and evaluate the range and effectiveness of the current curriculum provision for mathematics? What is the timescale for routine monitoring of the curriculum and who is responsible for carrying it out? How are they expected to manage this work?

15 **Development plan**

In broad terms what are the plans for further development of the mathematics curriculum?

16 **Review**

At what date will this policy statement be reviewed?

Most schools are working towards the full coverage of these policy areas. An effective policy identifies what is being done now, and shows, in relation to the school development plan, how the school team is managing the curriculum development process over a two to three year period.

Organising the review and revision of policy documents

Policy documents can easily become dated in the current climate of rapid change. A review will be needed when current documents: have reached their review date; no longer reflect school aims; no longer describe current practice; cease to be of use to existing or new members of teaching and support staff.

One way of reviewing an existing policy statement with the whole staff

1 Circulate a copy of the current policy to all teaching staff. Think about who else to include (e.g. support staff, volunteers, parent governors). Highlight a particular section for them to work on in detail. Design and attach a simple grid for them to organise their responses.

2 Collate their replies and present these at a meeting on a large (A1) sheet so that strengths and weaknesses stand out clearly. Look for, accept and highlight contradictions: e.g. 'I think the section on special needs is too short and lacking detail,' 'I think the SEN section is too long and too elaborate.' Contradictions offer good opportunities for discussion and collaboration. They are a quick way to get to a deeper level of beliefs and needs. A focus for a meeting could be: 'How can we accommodate and integrate the different views expressed?' Meetings need to be managed so that individuals don't feel they are under pressure to withdraw their viewpoint.

3 If no joint meeting is planned, circulate a summary of results to everyone along with an explanation and a timetable of your next few steps. You need to make sure you're available on occasions for those who have second thoughts and need to talk to you. Some people (e.g. a newly qualified teacher, a part time teacher, learning support staff) may have valuable ideas to contribute but may not be sufficiently confident to offer them in a large meeting. They may be willing to offer useful thoughts privately.

4 Schools are hierarchical in their power structures and this can limit the opportunity to express ideas that run

counter to current beliefs and practice. There is always a risk that differences of opinion are not discussed sufficiently for quality ideas to emerge. Those with the most power may insist on what they want and those who see themselves as having the least power may acquiesce. This may occur even though experience tells us that the most powerful people in the group don't have a monopoly of the best ideas. Second, groups of people are more likely to understand complex issues when they've been through a cycle of: stating their opinions; acknowledging disagreement; accepting and clarifying the difference between their ideas; and tolerating differences in order to get the task completed.

5   Invite another person to collaborate with you on writing up the general response to the current policy. Remember that reviewing a policy doesn't mean it **has** to be re-written: 'If it ain't broken, don't try to mend it!'

6   Look at other policies in existence in the school. Are there similarities of content and style? Does the special nature of mathematics require a maths policy that looks different and contains different information from others? Does the maths policy reflect the aims and ethos of the school? Are there consistencies with other policies in terms of what is being written about; (e.g. equal opportunities, social, moral and cultural development, homework policy, marking and assessment procedures)? What other themes need to run through all the school policies in order to show a consistency of approach?

7   You may like to use the following grid as part of the review process. Expand it to A4 and circulate to all those on your list. Expect some colleagues to come to you with queries. An efficient use of time in a large school is to arrange to visit colleagues when they meet in small working groups and get them to fill out a copy while you wait. That puts them under pressure to complete quickly. Collect the questionnaires in and offer colleagues the opportunity to come to you later with additional comments, but give a deadline.

Some of the most helpful comments will come from coordinators of other subjects who are most likely to spot differences between your policy and the policy for their subject.

Name_____	What I like about the current policy.	What I don't like about the current policy.	What I think should be included in a new version.
General comments			
My views on the particular section you asked me to look at (**you** write the section title here before circulation).			

Running a workshop to develop a policy document

1 Study the headings provided above and modify them to suit your situation. Decide how to distribute the headings or how people will choose a heading to work on. Stress to them that you need their views, and differences of opinion need to be welcomed and regarded as important. Advice and suggestions are needed because it is impossible for a coordinator to know everything. Avoid having your workshop tacked onto a business meeting. Stick to time. Start and stop at the agreed times whether work is finished or not.

2 Arrange for some staff workshop time if this is possible. Make it clear to colleagues that they will be expected to tackle practical tasks and to write — not just listen.

Alternatively, send out copies of a worksheet containing one or more headings and some working instructions. Set a date for completion and return to you.

If your school is large and people regularly meet in phase or year groups then allow them sufficient time for a couple of meetings before the finished worksheet is to be returned to you. If you work in a small school, it might be better to manage the work over three or four meetings of the whole staff and to start by tackling some of the easier headings first.

3 If you run a workshop, use the headings to provide a focus for discussion. Share out the headings and allow small groups to discuss ideas together using a large flipchart sheet. After twenty minutes interrupt and review the sheets. Allow another ten minutes more if needed and get posters into a clear format.

4 Get people to display posters on walls or tables, walk around and look at them, serve tea. Finish by explaining what you will do with the information. Invite people to contribute other ideas informally over the next few days as they think of additional things. Thank colleagues for their contribution and tell them what will happen next. Invite help with sorting out what will be produced. Close the workshop.

Later

Write up a short statement under each of the headings that people tackled. Use notes you take during the workshop or passed to you from members of each group, or from the poster sheets that you collect after the workshop. Circulate your written notes to colleagues at a later date for further comment, modification and final agreement.

Each of your chosen headings together with the finally agreed wording will form sections of your policy statement.

Chapter 13

Long-term planning

A school's long-term planning could involve three termly sheets for each class which contains a single age-group. The whole school could work on a fortnightly topic cycle. Each fortnight could consist of a *number* topic and another drawn from one of the other Programmes of Study. The teaching fortnight could be arranged as 10 hourly lessons: 6 of number, 2 of topic work and 2 using investigations to support *using and applying*. The resulting sheets would look like those below in Figure 13.1.

Some schools develop much of their mathematics from topic work in other curriculum areas, like history or RE. A large junior school might decide to have a termly topic cycle. Mathematics is taught for five lessons each week: three lessons develop from the topic and two are focused on number and do not relate directly to the topic work. The school might take its whole school topic titles from RE. The resulting long-term planning sheet might then look like Figure 13.2, with activities for mathematics determined by the whole school topic. The actual activities for each year group are given in detail in the school's related medium-term planning sheets. Thus, work identified in these sheets for the autumn term as **weight**, **height**, etc. will be detailed in the medium-term sheets showing differentiated work that provides a range of activities suitable for each age group.

AUTUMN TERM	Number work	Topic work	Problem solving and investigation
Week 1	place value	weight	investigating doubling and halving
2	place value	weight	solving a weight problem as part of D&T work
3	addition and subtraction	shape and space	number investigation using sequences of addition and subtraction
4	addition and subtraction	shape and space	shape investigation
5			
6			

SPRING TERM	Number work	Topic work	Problem solving and investigation
Week 1	place value	volume and capacity	place value investigation
2	place value	volume and capacity	practical problem solving task on volume
3	money	graphs	problem solving with money
4	money	graphs	number investigation
5			
6			

SUMMER TERM	Number work	Topic work	Problem solving and investigation
Week 1	place value using calculators	shape and space	calculator investigation
2	place value using calculators	shape and space	shape investigation
3	multiplication and division	area	number investigation
4	multiplication and division	area	area investigation
5			
6			

FIG 13.1
Long term planning — termly sheets

YEAR I of a two YEAR ROLLING PROGRAMME	Autumn	Spring	Summer
RE	Myself and others	Exploring books	Exploring the world
Maths across the curriculum	Making decisions shape weight height data handling	Maths from stories — (Noah's Ark) symmetry, (Islamic patterns) Reasoning	Length Direction Scales and ratios
PE	Partner work and co-operation stretching and curling swimming dance		
Music	performing: with friends, singing songs, using IT, composing: voice and instruments with changing emphasis . . . listening/appraising: songs about friendship		

Generally, the long-term planning ensures coverage of the National Curriculum and provides guidance on the balance to be achieved over each term and each year.

Doing the long-term planning collaboratively

Sitting together and planning a yearly programme for mathematics topics does not have to be a lengthy task. Many schools have adopted a whole school approach to this level of planning. What is increasingly being seen as vital if long-term planning is to become more effective and efficient is that planning groups need access to a mathematics coordinator who can quickly outline how a general topic label like 'algebra' can be broken down in a detailed way into a possible sequence of relevant and pleasurable experiences for children from 4-11 and their teachers. This demands a much greater knowledge of the mathematics curriculum than coordinators were expected to demonstrate prior to the National Curriculum. It is not a reflection of teacher inadequacy but a sign of increased expectation emerging from the recognised need for children to acquire a greater understanding of mathematics.

One of the advantages of joint planning of the mathematics curriculum is that it leads to more effective management of resources and to financial savings. It is possible to achieve better control over continuity and progression both within and between classes. For example, when teachers at Key Stage 1 carry out the first round of their planning, it is possible that *length* appears in the summer term of Y1 but doesn't appear again until the spring of Y2. When using this style of planner, the timing of topics can be immediately altered to produce a more appropriate programme.

Long-term planning documents often list the science, geography and history topics planned to be taught over a predetermined cycle; often of two, three or four years, depending on the size and type of school. The duration of the topics is also shown and this again can differ from school to school: a term in some cases, a half term or less in others. In some schools, planning for mathematics is presented quite separately from the rest of the long-term planning. In others, all the subjects appear as topics and are present in the same planning document. Schools have developed various arrangements for the long-term planning of mathematics. There are advantages and disadvantages in keeping mathematics separate from other curriculum areas and from seeking some form of integration. The issues are complex and are explored below, starting with the loosest form of linkage that is currently found in schools.

Loose integration between maths and other subjects

In this plan, mathematics is detailed separately and the format may well be quite different from that used for the other subjects. The mathematics curriculum may be detailed as a list of books associated with a commercially published scheme. Little attempt is made to link the work in mathematics with that in the other subjects and this often reflects the predominant teaching style in the school where mathematics is taught as a separate subject. The acquisition of knowledge and skills developed in science, history, geography, design and technology etc. is not closely linked to the work in mathematics. The long-term planning for mathematics lists the books to be used by each year group, details the publisher's list of recommended and required equipment and resources and extends it to include resources that the school has built up on its own initiative.

Advantages

Where the current practice in a school is to teach National Curriculum subjects separately there is little point in spending time identifying links at a planning level that will not be exploited in practice. Detailing the mathematics content is less complex when maths is taught separately. Where the current practice is to teach a discrete number of lessons each week for a known period of time, it is less difficult for teachers to assess whether there is sufficient teaching time available to cover the mathematics listed in the long-term planning. If the school bases most of the work on commercially produced mathematics materials then the structure of the commercial scheme(s) can be seen as defining the curriculum. Familiarity with a scheme that has been in use for a few years will already have allowed teachers to identify gaps and weaknesses. The more enterprising will have dealt with these problems by looking for additional resources or seeking advice from the coordinator. Part of the coordinator's role is to ensure that colleagues cover the topics in sufficient depth so that children have some continuity of experience and there is a progressive development of mathematical ideas and skills as children progress through the school. The curriculum plan either accepts the single route dictated by some schemes or identifies an agreed pathway through the available material. More recent schemes have built-in assessment activities and suggestions for record-keeping, extension and consolidation designed to provide work of different levels of difficulty.

Disadvantages

The often high-quality long-term planning in the other subjects may not be reflected in the planning for mathematics. Long-term plans in the other subjects, like art, history, geography and RE, for example, often very carefully outline the teacher's role when introducing new topics; actively teaching new skills. The way the teacher is expected to help children explore new areas of knowledge is often quite clearly defined, especially in subjects like design and technology. In mathematics, the teacher's role is often less detailed and a passive role is often assumed or emerges in consequence. In the worst situations, during the time when children work on mathematics, the teacher is actively engaged in teaching another curriculum area.

Mathematics is a core subject which takes a large and increasing proportion of curriculum time. The subject and the children deserve and require that teachers take a role at least as active as that in other curriculum areas.

Opportunities for involving children in practical work in mathematics lessons are frequently missed in situations where the scheme books are seen to be the appropriate vehicle for the introduction of new topics and skills. Where this occurs lessons can become static and aimless, determined by the pace of the children working through the pages. Most crucially, **discussion** — an essential ingredient in children's learning, can disappear. Children's acquisition of knowledge and skills may be measured not through understanding but quantitatively through the number of pages and books completed. The levels of misunderstanding and gaps in knowledge fail to emerge until well after the event.

The National Curriculum for mathematics is still overloaded. There is an immense amount to cover especially at Key Stage 2. It is not necessary for a child to meet a mathematics learning objective only in a mathematics lesson. Indeed, it is virtually impossible to exclude work in measures, data handling and number from the work children cover in art, design and technology, science, geography and history for example. Organising topics so that data collection in science is taught in conjunction with data handling and interpretation in mathematics makes sense in terms of managing an overloaded mathematics curriculum as well as being educationally effective.

Trying to change teaching styles by modifying the style of the mathematics long-term planning is not a strategy that is likely to change the current practice if that is the intention. Colleagues will file the planning and continue to work in ways that are familiar and comfortable. Encouraging changes in practice will not come from bold statements of insistence in long-term planning documents.

Linking mathematics with other subjects

In this plan, the structure of the long-term planning bears close comparison with the model on p. 166 but with closer links between mathematics and the other subjects. This is often achieved when the maths coordinator works in conjunction with other subject coordinators to explore the topics that form the rolling programme of science or humanities subjects. In many schools one subject provides the major topic for a term or half term.

The coordinators identify key concepts, skills and attitudes in the major topic and find equivalents in the other work that could be taught during that same period. Having identified areas of mathematics that could be taught in support of the major topic these links are recorded and the mathematics programme begins to emerge in response to the other subjects in a way which also ensures that it retains an internal coherence as well as playing a supportive role in the teaching of other subjects.

Advantages

If the planning reflects current practice and emerges from it, then children's experiences are likely to be more coherent. All subjects benefit from active teaching and the mathematics curriculum is at different times a useful tool in exploring other subjects, a medium for communication of facts and ideas as well as a source of study in its own right, provided the coordinator ensures that some topics are included which allow exploration of mathematics for its own sake. Maths is likely to be seen as relevant because it is regularly used to help gain access to other knowledge and concepts relating to other curriculum areas. With this level of integration, maths coordinators and their colleagues are much less likely to be constrained by the structure of a commercial mathematics scheme. They are more likely to select elements of their adopted curriculum programme to support the work in other subjects. A feeling of professional freedom and responsibility is more likely to emerge as teachers recognise that they can select the most appropriate mathematical experiences for their children.

Disadvantages

The idea that everything must be linked is both naïve and counter-productive. There are topics in all subjects which are worthy of independent study at some time and the spurious production of tenuous links is self-defeating. Where there are few opportunities to study maths for its own sake there is a danger that maths lessons can disappear from the timetable to be replaced with a 'topic' label. Both the timetable and the mathematics teaching can lack clarity, precision and focus.

At worst, maths can be taught incidentally and irregularly under a global heading called 'topic' which is never defined within the school and which carries very different meanings for different teachers. When time boundaries are not kept and the time taken to carry out the main topic work in science, technology or whatever is not well managed and escalates, then the time for maths may evaporate and large areas of the maths curriculum may not get the time they require.

The complexity demanded by this level of planning may not be appropriate for a school. It should follow not lead, changes in teaching style. If the long-term planning does not reflect carefully organised lessons, then it is difficult to ensure continuity between different classes in the same year group. Children's experience of the whole curriculum and of mathematics in particular becomes an accident determined by the class to which they are allocated. Although we are not looking for identical experiences in parallel classes, nor are we suggesting that lessons in parallel classes should be duplicates, it is essential that children's access to the curriculum is broadly similar across a year group.

It is unproductive for coordinators to push their colleagues from a situation where there are loose links between maths and other subjects, towards a situation where subjects are more closely tied together. Some colleagues may not be convinced about the value of giving up the authority of the published scheme. Others may not have sufficient experience of other teaching styles to be able to adopt them at short notice. Some teachers do not welcome changes in the way maths is taught because the proposed changes threaten to fundamentally undermine current working practices in other subjects. Crucially, some teachers need maths to be a passive book-based routine because they have failed to find ways of creating opportunities to carry other important tasks like listening to children read, or taking a small group of special needs children for in-depth work. A teacher who routinely uses a commercial workbook or worksheet scheme to keep children 'occupied' while they teach another curriculum area faces a major disruption to the whole of their classroom organisation if they are asked to transform mathematics from a passive, book-based activity into a highly interactive teacher-led subject.

While I would argue strongly that when children are learning maths the teacher should be actively teaching maths, teachers would be wise to resist demands for sweeping changes to their classroom practice until they are convinced the change will be worthwhile and that they are going to get strong and positive support in managing the required change.

Chapter 14

Medium-term planning

Introduction

Medium-term planning is used to ensure coverage of the Programmes of Study and Learning Objectives. It matches NC curriculum statements to appropriate activities and resources, including IT, for children. It is often organised to demonstrate the school has planned for continuity and progression and is written in sufficient detail to provide teachers with a scheme of work.

Suggested sheets for medium-term planning

This type of layout has been tried by many schools and commercially produced versions are available from several LEAs. The order in which learning objectives appear is usually hierarchical with increasingly difficult ideas introduced as one reads each sheet from top to bottom. This arrangement best suits mathematics when taught as a separate subject. Sheets are often A3 size and some schools organise the sheets to show clearly those which are associated with each year group. The actual layout depends on the school — a two class school with 4–7 year olds in a single classroom requires a different arrangement of medium-term planning sheets to that required by a two-form entry school (see Figure 14.1).

FIG 14.1
Example of a medium-term
planning sheet

Learning Objectives	Suggested activities	Available resources	Links and references to IT software, and commercial material

FIG 14.2
Suggested topic plan sheet

Topic — Homes and Habitats: Using the school grounds to explore homes built by a variety of creatures			
Learning Objectives	Suggested activities	Available resources	Links and references to IT software, and commercial material

© Falmer Press Ltd

Broadly the same format can be used by a school where mathematics forms part of series of topics. Each sheet is associated with the topic and includes information about trips, journeys etc. that are planned to develop mathematics from the topic work. Each sheet can relate to a class or year group or to the whole school. The format will vary according to how the school decides to support the required differentiation. The planning format can then look something like the example in Figure 14.2.

Some schools have adopted very different layouts. One alternative that is very economical of space requires rewriting the NC learning objectives onto separate sheets of A4 broken down into the different parts of each Programme of Study. For example, *Shape, space and measures* is broken down into separate sheets which show learning objectives for *movement*, *location* and *measurement*. Each section is then further sub-divided to provide a sheet for a single class or year group. The work identified by the school to be covered by a single class or year group is presented on a single sheet. In this way, coverage of the NC is clearly demonstrated. It is not until they produce their short-term, weekly planning, that teachers identify groups of children, activities and resources.

Commercial medium-term planning material

Schools that have chosen to buy and trial medium-term planning materials tend to keep the originals in good condition and, in the first year, photocopy and modify selected sheets that become the basis for the school's version. Medium-term planning sheets are selected by referring to the long-term, topic-based planning which identifies the topics to be covered during a particular period. Initially, groups of teachers might find it useful to work together to produce a common format and working routine. Plans should be prepared at least a term in advance. The most urgent issue in most schools is to find ways of reducing this lengthy process to one that is quick, efficient and informative. Efforts centre round finding a format for originals that is sufficiently flexible to allow teachers to change some of the activities they use from one year to the next without having to reproduce a new base sheet. A basic set of sheets that can be photocopied annually allows highlighter pens to be used to select particular topics each year. If the sheets have been trialled and redesigned by the staff of the school and in addition have created plenty of white space on each sheet, then during this planning stage teachers can also add to the photocopy additional, favourite activities. Because this is potentially a very creative stage in curriculum planning, teachers might find it valuable to carry out this work at a joint planning meeting. This also serves to avoid unnecessary duplication of activities in different classes and is likely to ensure more effective monitoring of progression and continuity. It is a key meeting for the coordinator to attend: whether as a curriculum leader in a key stage or year group where they have plenty of experience, or in a more co-ordinating role where they are not very familiar with the teaching at this particular key stage or year group.

The medium-term planning sheets link the National Curriculum learning objectives with suggested activities and (when adapted after being tested in the school for a year or so) also show links to the school's equipment and resources including software and they effectively form the basis of a **scheme of work** and are known as such in many schools. It is the medium-term plan that identifies:

- which National Curriculum learning objectives are being focused on;
- which activities the planning team have selected as useful, and;
- which resources are needed to support the activities.

The medium-term plans should provide the class teacher with a range of activities from which to choose. The teacher should be able to select activities that support the full range of abilities within the class, although the actual arrangement of specific groups of children will only appear on the teacher's short-term planning.

Medium-term planning sheets need to be designed so that the teaching arrangements can easily and clearly be shown. A poorly designed sheet causes immense problems. In some classrooms groups of children tackle different areas of maths during the same lesson. For example, one group may be working at a sand/water tray filling and emptying containers of different shapes and sizes. At the same time in another part of the classroom others may be working on a table-top activity using a worksheet to practise forming numerals correctly. Another group may be making potato prints to produce a repeating pattern for a display. The layout of the school's medium-term planning sheets is vitally important. They should support the different styles of teaching found in the school. Poorly designed sheets that don't support the teaching, force teachers to continually modify them, rewriting substantial amounts of information in what is a most inefficient use of teachers' time.

Recently there has been a move away from the style of working outlined in the previous paragraph, where very different mathematical activities are being provided by the teacher during the same lesson. Increasingly, teachers are planning lessons and sequences of lessons that focus on a single mathematical topic. Differentiation is provided by modifying the chosen tasks within the single topic to meet the different levels of ability, age and aptitude of the children within the class. Teachers who have made this change to a single topic argue that the new approach helps them to:

- focus more effectively on teaching mathematical ideas;
- engage in more active teaching;
- create situations in the classroom where there are more opportunities for discussion;
- bring the whole class together if they so choose;
- get every child to contribute to whole-class discussion.

Teachers find it easier to create more time for talk **about maths** with less talking needed about classroom organisation. Teachers claim they spend less time telling children what they should be doing, and more time 'talking mathematics and big ideas'. A further advantage of a sharper focus is that the demands on resources can be predicted more easily. For example, demand for computer software to support maths may be integrated more effectively into the teaching programme. Commercially published schemes have useful resource lists that often suggest what might be included in a basic set of classroom resources. The curriculum need not end up becoming narrower or over-formalised as a result of this approach. It shouldn't be read as an attempt to reduce opportunities for practical activity, or a way of introducing more formal work. Too narrow a focus on basic skills of number to the detriment of a broad mathematics education is **not** an automatic consequence of a sharper focus within each lesson.

Completing the medium-term planning is a highly complex activity involving a large number of factors — many of which must be retained in the mind as the planning takes place. Many of the circumstances that affect medium-term planning change year by year, preventing the establishment of a smooth regular process, (e.g. the loss or gain of a class due to fluctuations in number on role, and especially the creation or disappearance of a class with a Y2/Y3 split). In consequence, the medium-term planning in many schools is still inefficiently carried out. Teachers too often are forced to start with a blank sheet of paper each year. Many have either to copy out long sections of the National Curriculum or resort to the use of coded letters and numbers which mean little to supply teachers and other colleagues who have to take their class at short notice. There is clearly a need for simplifying the planning as much and as quickly as possible so that the teachers' powers of creativity and inventiveness are saved for use in the classroom and the repeated copying of information from one format to another is reduced to an absolute minimum.

To summarise, effective medium-term planning, appropriately modified to meet the needs of a particular school:
- demonstrates clear and obvious links with the long-term planning;
- allows the teacher to identify which parts of the *Programme of Study* are being worked on during the period covered by the medium-term plan;
- shows the teacher what practical resources including IT are available;
- offers the teacher a choice of practical activities appropriate for supporting children as they work on the topic — including possible starting points for investigations and problem solving;

- indicates relevant pages and sections of commercially produced resources including work book and worksheet material for the practise and consolidation of knowledge and skills;
- indicates relevant pages of teacher handbooks and guides so that sources of background knowledge are easily located;
- suggests activities that can be used for assessment purposes;
- is structured so that planning is sufficiently clear and straightforward for a supply teacher to use if there is an unplanned absence;
- is sufficiently detailed to allow teachers to review a previous year's work and make improvements;
- shows the teacher what to teach next.

Making connections between schemes of work, medium-term plans and resources

It cannot be emphasised too strongly, that coordinators of mathematics should avoid agreeing to write a scheme of work on their own or largely single-handed. A scheme of work needs to emerge from a review of current beliefs and practice. It should support the planning and teaching of mathematics throughout the school. It is a highly complex and elaborate document containing guidance for all teachers and mirroring the current practice. It can only be completed when the school's current practice is known publicly and is available to be drawn on. The success of a scheme of work can be measured by the extent to which people say, 'How did we manage without it?'

Producing a scheme of work is a major task and in many schools the complete task may well be a two year project. So, what will it contain and what will it look like? It is very easy to produce vast and unwieldy documents — especially if this is the first time a school is in the process of producing its own scheme: though this may be an inevitable stage of growth and development. A scheme which is cumbersome and over-detailed rarely provides effective support for teachers to plan efficiently and creatively. At the end of the day, the quality of mathematics teaching should be raised significantly by the development and use of a new scheme. Producing it may not feel like a creative act, but the result should liberate colleagues and increase their confidence and enjoyment of teaching mathematics. That, and higher quality experiences for children are the prime objectives in developing a scheme of work.

Medium-term planning documents that are developed along the lines outlined above, form a substantial portion of a scheme of work. Schemes of work should either provide the essential information directly or indicate where it can be obtained elsewhere in the school's documentation. In particular the medium-term planning has been developed into a scheme of work when it shows:

- how the teaching of the subject contributes to the aims and ethos of the school as set out in the school's brochures and general policy documents;
- the way that **current practice** defines and directs subject policy as detailed in the subject policy document, and how current teaching of the subject has contributed to proposed developments in teaching;
- how teachers are expected to use the long-term, medium-term and short-term planning;
- what individual teachers and teaching groups are required to do when they plan, teach and evaluate their work;
- a programme of activities for children that meets National Curriculum requirements and other legislation;
- links between the chosen subject content, skills and attitudes and the specific learning objectives of the National Curriculum;
- areas of content that will be taught in relation to the age and Key Stage of the children, including how work with children in the early years relates to 'areas of experience' detailed in Desirable Outcomes;
- links between learning objectives, selected activities and the school's resources including IT;
- how resources may be deployed to full advantage in providing all children with access to the full curriculum;
- the way in which children with very different needs will be catered for;
- how equal access and equal opportunity will be provided and preserved;
- how teachers will be deployed and children organised into teaching and learning groups;
- what range of teaching styles will be employed;

- what expectations, in general terms, the staff hold for the performance of the children;
- how the cycle of planning, implementation and evaluation of the teaching programme is monitored;
- where responsibility for the effective teaching of the subject lies and how this carried out;
- how the cycle of teaching, learning and the informal and formal assessment of children's performance informs future teaching plans and how this cycle leads into formal record-keeping, reporting to parents and other outside agencies;
- links with outside bodies, the local community and the world of work;
- how the school's senior management team and the governors exercise their responsibilities.

For many schools the scheme of work is a single document. For others it is better produced as a collection of booklets.

Availability of resources

There is a strong link between the development of medium-term planning, its steady expansion into a scheme of work and the whole issue of availability and deployment of resources. An audit of existing resources is absolutely essential because it can save substantial sums of money and it allows for future expenditure to be better planned and targeted. The decision to carry out an audit should be a joint one but getting everyone to accept may be the head's responsibility. It often requires an amnesty as part of the same process.

There are likely to be problems with implementing the school's scheme of work if:
- there is a history of class teachers having their own yearly allowance which has been spent independently of any advice or guidance from a coordinator;
- there is wide variation in what is available in different classrooms;
- if there is wide variation in teaching styles and the way in which equipment is used throughout the school,
- if centralised resources have been badly maintained in the past.

The mapping of resources to the medium-term planning will inevitably show up some form of mismatch. The mismatch may be because resources exist but no clear use for them appears on the newly drafted planning sheets (such bits and pieces as Stern apparatus, clinometers and Cuisenaire rods may all be available but some teachers may be unsure about their use). Bringing resources back into use may require some research into current practice, perhaps some inservice training or the provision of some specific classroom activities. The help of a local maths consultant or LEA advisory staff may be needed.

An obvious mismatch occurs when a lack of appropriate resources prevents teachers from using activities identified in the scheme of work. An audit should clarify whether there are stockpiles of equipment in a single teacher's storage cupboard. You may eventually decide to buy more of a particular resource but this should only come after a decision to deploy existing stocks more widely has been rejected. Another mismatch emerges when the resources are insufficient to meet peak demand. One possibility is to review where topics occur in the long-term and medium-term plans: it may not be essential for everyone to be 'doing capacity' at the same time. Peak demand for resources can be smoothed out by changing the order in which topics are taught through the school. Looking for ways to spread demand more evenly throughout the year is a very economical way of ensuring adequate resources when budgets are tight providing children with the maximum opportunity to become skilled users of essential equipment through regular practise. (See Chapter 10 for more information.) It is financially foolish to insist that the school spends large sums in order to make sufficient resources available for a high demand that lasts three weeks in the school year and which is followed by under-use for the rest of the time.

Using maths schemes — points to consider

Commercially produced materials deserve special attention. These resources have a strong influence on teaching styles, learning opportunities and classroom organisation. Teachers need to be fully aware of the content of teachers' and pupils' materials, especially workbooks, textbooks and worksheets. The pupils' workbooks and textbooks often present a couple of pages of shape work, followed by some work on fractions, then some addition or subtraction practice. This scattering of the content poses problems for teachers who need to assess the content in terms of breadth, depth, and progression. One solution is to cut up two copies and staple together the related pages, forming sets of pages covering each topic. The quality of the workbook and textbook pages can then be assessed and decisions made about which pages to use and which ones to supplement with other materials.

Of course, it is not necessary to cut up the children's own textbooks and workbooks. Once the teachers' own copies have been reassembled, it is easy to direct the children to specific pages. For example, the teacher will have seen from the long-term planning that for the next two weeks the class will be working on the topic of Time. The teacher will have reviewed the relevant pages in the medium-term plans which show the practical activities suggested. The relevant pages of the commercial scheme are also shown and the teacher can direct the children to these pages in order to practise and consolidate the topic after the practical work has been done. In summary, there are a number of important points to consider when evaluating commercial maths scheme resources.

1 Look at continuity and progression within the pages and decide what to do about inappropriate development of ideas.
2 Look at gaps — too little probability, too much computation practice, for the most and least able.
3 Review the extent to which the scheme provides coverage of the National Curriculum PoS.
4 Review the support for teacher assessment within the scheme.
5 Put written references into the medium-term planning package provided by the LEA showing where the newly stapled collections of pages support the learning objectives.
6 Begin to add teacher's own preferred practical activities to the learning objectives, (in addition to those already supplied on the LEA medium-term sheets).

7 Change teaching styles in classrooms so that children no longer work through the scheme books page by page.

Storage of equipment and resources

Storage of equipment and resources is a very individual matter for each school. The layout of the building, the ability to keep central storage areas maintained with the minimum of fuss, an easy way of monitoring who has resources — all contribute to decisions about how and where to store materials. The learning objectives in *using and applying* PoS strongly hint that children should have easy access to materials and resources so that they can demonstrate an increasing ability to select appropriate materials to carry out tasks.

For medium-term planning to be effective the role of commercially produced workbook and worksheet schemes has to be reviewed and in some cases changed. They can be useful in providing consolidation and practise of knowledge and skills that have been introduced and taught by the teacher. By redefining their role as a source of activities to consolidate what has already been introduced by the teacher, it follows that the order of the topics within a workbook or worksheet scheme should not be what determines the order of the mathematical topics taught to children. This is a professional judgment to be reserved for teachers and should emerge from the production of long-term and medium-term planning.

Many of the more recently published schemes have a desk top folder with copious suggestions for each topic, including a range of activities for children, advice on classroom organisation and background mathematical information for those unsure of the mathematics. Each topic is a sequence of lessons and can be lifted out of the main folder and a sequence or pathway for the year devised by the teacher well beforehand. It is easy to be overwhelmed by the sheer quantity of material offered but it is possible to remain in control of the commercial material if the teacher starts from the school's medium-term planning sheets and then selects some of the activities, worksheets and textbook pages to support the teaching.

Chapter 15 | Short-term planning

Introduction

In the weekly planning sheet shown in Figure 15.1, the two sides of the same A3 sheet are designed to make enough space for five days for the core subjects. A similar sheet provides space for the other foundation subjects and RE.

Teachers complete these sheets a week in advance of the lessons. Information is drawn from the medium-term planning sheet for the period in question. Copies of the medium-term sheets can be marked using highlighter pens. There should be a minimum of copying the same words from medium-term to short-term sheets. The front of the weekly planning sheet needs to be completed to indicate how specific activities are being matched to groups of children. There is space for notes to be made about infrequently used or centrally stored resources. The sheets incorporate opportunities for assessment to inform future planning.

The learning objectives that the teacher has selected for monitoring children's significant achievement are transferred from the medium-term sheet. The best opportunities for assessment are often brief informal episodes during the lesson. Children can be monitored most effectively during lessons which include open-ended investigations and problem solving. The children's significant achievement can also be monitored by normal questioning and discussion, or

FRONT   REVERSE

WEEKLY PLAN FOR CLASS ____ YEAR GROUP ____ TERM _____ DATE _____	LEARNING OBJECTIVES	RESOURCES / NOTES	OPPORTUNITIES FOR ASSESSMENT: IDENTIFYING SIGNIFICANT ACHIEVEMENT NAME OF TARGET GROUP INDIVIDUAL CHILDREN NAMED AS NECESSARY	Date
ENGLISH				
MATHS				
SCIENCE				

FIG 15.1
Example of a weekly planning sheet

obtained from scrutiny of children's workbooks. The most useful opportunities arise during practical situations because learning objectives which relate to *using and applying* can be assessed at the same time as the acquisition of content objectives. Not all learning objectives will be assessed. Monitoring four key objectives per term with each target group is a realistic way to begin.

During the short periods when the target group is being monitored, the right-hand edge of the sheet can be folded over to bring the section 'Opportunities for assessment: Identifying significant achievement' from the back to the front. The teacher monitors one group of children for brief periods, but only makes written notes about significant achievement and significant difficulties. Notes are not made here of children making steady and expected progress. Comments on the actual difficulties and breakthroughs experienced by individual children in the target group can be made in the notes section.

When the teacher completes the short-term planning for the coming week, the next set of activities can be identified from the medium-term plans in the usual way, but the short-term planning is informed by, develops from and incorporates, the assessment notes written on the sheet from the previous week. Assessment must inform future planning so that children do not receive a rigid diet of activities taken from the medium-term plans. Short-term planning must be influenced by the assessments made in previous weeks in order to respond to children's needs.

Teaching is a creative process where teachers' ideas are turned into experiences for children. Teachers keep many of their ideas stored in the mind: thoughts about how best to support children; thoughts about the best way to use a parent who has volunteered help; wondering about the most effective way of introducing a new piece of software; deciding how to make the best use of time. The list is endless and since primary school teachers rarely have non-contact time in which to prepare and refine planning, it is likely that too much is carried in the head.

The introduction of a National Curriculum has changed many aspects of the planning process. Perhaps the biggest change is the requirement that planning throughout the school should be harmonised so that continuity and progression of the curriculum is both provided and is seen to be provided. For this to happen, plans have to be in a form that communicates this whole school approach both to the teachers within the school and to others from outside.

It is evident from the range of planning devices that have been generated in schools recently that there is no single solution. Where schools have been over-prescriptive in detailing the layout of the short-term plans, there are often problems for individual teachers. People think, write, plan and see connections between ideas in different ways. Some people operate effectively with lists of jobs to do. Others need a more spatially organised set of words, pictures and arrows to represent their ideas and their teaching intentions. The degree of comfort we experience when working with different formats — lists, diagrams, arrows — is part of our individual make-up. So, being asked to draw up plans of our ideas in a way that is inappropriate for our style of thinking actually gets in the way of the ideas themselves. Having said this, there needs to be agreement about what information the short-term planning sheet will contain and what level of detail is appropriate.

When considering the development of the short-term planning, consider whether the format(s) adopted:

- makes clear sense to other readers particularly job-share colleagues, non-teaching assistants and supply staff;
- contains the appropriate information to the level of detail agreed;
- allows long-term and medium-term plans to be turned into effective lessons;
- matches activities to identified groups and, where necessary, to individual children;
- identifies opportunities for informal and formal assessment of children's performance;
- supports teaching over a period of time so that series of lessons are coherent and provide consolidation, practise and extension;
- shows a broad and appropriate range of quality experiences for children;
- demonstrates that lessons meet legislative requirements, including curriculum coverage, pupil entitlement, equal opportunities, etc.;
- shows how teaching, learning, and resources are to be integrated;
- shows the deployment of the teacher and other adults and the management of SEN and able pupil groups.

Chapter 16

Monitoring the planning

The coordinator must try to keep an overview of the planning, not just at the writing and development stages, but also later when the planning is in operation and doing its job of supporting teachers. What follows is a look at planning from different viewpoints. Because the planning process is so complex, you may need to focus on one aspect of planning at a time in order to see what whole school picture emerges. There are many aspects you could choose to focus on. Some of them are described below. The examples are:

1 time constraints;
2 what needs to be included for the planning to be complete;
3 the range of responsibilities;
4 classroom organisation and management;
5 using mental work to develop numeracy;
6 providing a broad range of learning experiences.

What are the time constraints?

1 Long-term — more than one year.
2 Medium-term — a term ahead.
3 Short-term — the next week or fortnight.
4 How much time is given to topics and how is this determined?
5 How much curriculum time does mathematics take, does it meet recommendations?
6 How is the allocation of time determined for mathematics within topic work throughout the different classes?
7 How is the allocation of time determined for mathematics as a separate subject?
8 How is the time distributed for mathematics between work in whole class, mixed groups, in ability groups, in sets formed across classes?
9 How is work in the different Programmes of Study planned so as to provide a balance?
10 How is the time balanced between different activities in maths: e.g. problem solving, investigations, discussion, individual work, the introduction of new ideas, practise and consolidation, oral and written work?

What is needed for the planning to be complete?

1 Broad topics to be covered with a class or group of classes over a year or more.
2 Activities differentiated for different abilities, specific resources, assessment opportunities and links across other curriculum subjects.
3 Named groups of children in class, specific times of day, fixed periods of time, different ways of teaching.
4 Advice about resources; their availability, usefulness, the strategies and techniques needed to use them effectively.
5 Advice about techniques needed for use with different teaching styles; active teaching to large groups, active teaching with small groups and individuals. Monitoring individual children's progress by observing small groups and the use of questioning to enquire about levels of understanding.
6 Classroom layout: many classrooms in other countries with high levels of success in teaching mathematics do not sit children together around small groups of tables but employ a horseshoe layout with the open end containing a large writing board and sufficient space for the teacher and individual children to come out and demonstrate their ideas. This provides the maximum opportunity for face-to-face discussion and eye contact.
7 Advice about the collection and use of informal and formal assessments, appropriate marking of children's work, feedback to children about achievement, feeding the results of assessments into future stages of the planning cycle.
8 Advice on helping children manage the experience of SATs.
9 Guidance on record-keeping, retaining appropriate data in an efficient form, portfolios of children's achievement, use of the school standards bank to help with the formal assessment process, children's records of achievement.
10 Advice about reporting to parents.

The range of responsibilities

1 The whole school agrees the order and frequency of broad topics to be covered and the time to be devoted to mathematics as a separate subject and as part of topic work.
2 Year group or phase group colleagues are responsible for balance between parallel classes, continuity within their own class, making sure time for maths meets agreed targets and they plan activities and resources together accordingly to ensure balance between Programmes of Study, the assessment points and activities.
3 Class teachers determine groups of children, the order of activities, the teaching styles and equality of access to children of different abilities, in consultation with the SENCO and other colleagues.
4 Coordinators monitor the planning done by phase groups and individual teachers, monitor the teaching in classrooms, the assessment opportunities and the results of assessment, the quality and quantity of resources, and the long-term, medium-term and day-to-day support for colleagues as they teach the subject. (This is a daunting list and just shows the extent to which ambitions for primary education are seldom matched by resources or opportunities.)

Classroom organisation and management

1 How much time is given to maths as a separate subject and to the mathematical part of topic work?
2 How much time is devoted to 'practical work' — do teachers agree on what they mean by the term?
3 Do children have opportunities for extended tasks lasting more than a couple of hours, tasks of short duration lasting a few minutes, tasks set by teachers, tasks they set themselves?
4 How do teachers introduce their lessons, link their lessons, review them?
5 Is good practice being disseminated through the school?
6 Is there consistent practice in the use of equipment and resources. Do children get increasing responsibility for looking after, selecting and finding effective ways of using equipment?
7 What sorts of opportunity do children get to talk, discuss, and debate their ideas and the ideas of other children in lessons?
8 What opportunities do children have to demonstrate their own methods and techniques?
9 Do children do their own target setting in maths?
10 How are lessons arranged to ensure a balance between the introduction of new ideas, practise and consolidation, development of strategies and techniques, assessment of knowledge, skills and understanding?
11 What variation is there between classes in the use of workbooks, textbooks, and worksheets? Can the variation be justified?
12 Are children of different abilities appropriately challenged by differentiated work, either within each class or within sets? Where children are grouped by ability for maths are the composition of the groups based on prior attainment or some other criteria that is likely to improve future attainment?
13 Do the methods of organisation make maths enjoyable and rewarding for teachers and children?

Using mental work to develop numeracy

1 Is there a policy, either separate or within the body of the scheme, for the development of numeracy including Desirable Outcomes for younger children?

2 Do children get regular opportunities to practise estimation and approximation in their oral work in class?

3 Are children regularly practising techniques like doubling and halving, rounding up and down to the nearest five, ten, twenty, fifty, hundred, etc., counting forwards and backwards in tens, twenties, fifties, hundreds, from different starting numbers?

4 Are children encouraged to invent and describe their own ways of finding the answers to mental additions and subtractions?

5 Are children taught to read number lines and number grids and encouraged to invent their ways of computing with them?

6 Do children use number lines to see addition as the combination of a starting point and a jump, e.g. to add 3 and 18, start on 18 and jump on 3.

7 Do they see subtraction as the difference between two numbers on a number line, usually found by counting on, e.g. the difference between 21 and 18 is found by counting from 18 to 21.

8 Do teachers spend time discussing simple relationships and patterns with children?

9 Can the children select their own mathematics for solving mental problems?

10 Can children discuss their own methods using mathematical language?

Providing children with a broad range of experiences

1 How do teachers through the school vary in their teaching styles when teaching mathematics?

2 Do experiences for children vary through the school? What differences are there between children's experiences *prior* to Key Stage 1, *at* Key Stage 1 and *at* Key Stage 2?

3 Do children get opportunities to work in whole class and small group situations with the teacher actively introducing new ideas, creating opportunities for discussion and demonstrating techniques?

4 Do children use and select resources, equipment and materials? Are different resources made available by teachers as children progress through the school? What are the reasons for the choice of different resources?

5 How does the balance between different ways of working vary across the school, e.g. using workbooks, textbooks and worksheets, practise and consolidation of previously learned work, learning maths in a topic, learning maths as a separate subject? What are the reasons for the variations between classes?

6 How much time do children get to demonstrate their own ways of working and to discuss strategies and techniques?

7 What do children experience when groupings for mathematics are changed? Have children's opinions been sought about the effects of different ways of grouping? Do teacher's and children's views and opinions match up?

8 What differences are there throughout the school in the way children are observed and assessed in maths? In what ways does marking vary? Are children involved in marking their own work, in discussion with their teacher about the strengths and weaknesses of their own work, in setting their own targets for improvement?

9 Do SATs results match what children should be achieving? Is this the case for low ability, average and high ability children? Do girls and boys achieve equally well? Are children from different ethnic groups equally successful? Can you identify where in the school, children make the most and the least progress in terms of their understanding, knowledge and skills?

The boxes above provide different starting points for reviewing your scheme of work. As part of any review:

1 Ask yourself *why* you are reviewing and developing your scheme — try to make a precise statement.

2 Write down a list of questions to which you need answers.

3 Write down a precise list of shortcomings that currently exist when teachers plan and implement the current scheme.

4 Write down a list of clearly identifiable targets that you need to achieve if you are to meet your goals.

5 How much common understanding is there between colleagues about the next development?

6 How much common agreement is there about how to further develop the·mathematics curriculum?

Many schools are at a point where schemes of work are still being developed and schools are still experimenting with aspects of the *planning, implementing* and *evaluating* cycle. We are likely to see demands for a significant increase in the time given over to numeracy and meeting these demands will require schools to continue to modify their planning and teaching over the next few years.

Points to consider when revising a scheme of work

For some schools, the revision process is prompted by the action plan that follows the OFSTED inspection and the identification of key issues to be addressed by the school. For many schools it is the School Development Plan that drives and guides the process of revising the scheme of work. An effective SDP is a transparent document that shows clearly how the identified needs of the school have been turned into a sequence of budgeted tasks. The SDP will identify the various stages of the revision of a scheme of work. It will set timetables, identify key individuals and their responsibilities and will have realistically earmarked time for staff meetings and professional days. It will identify simple ways of measuring success and the work will have been costed and budgets will have been identified to pay for such things as:

- temporary allocation of above-scale payments;
- non-contact time for coordinators and other key staff at various points;
- the buying in of advisory staff and consultants for clearly specified tasks;
- INSET provision for key people;
- increased secretarial time for producing final versions of documentation;
- purchase of resources to complement the anticipated scheme of work.

It is important not to waste time carrying out revisions that are unnecessary. The whole purpose of revising your scheme should be that it helps teachers improve their effectiveness and it raises children's attainment. If you are claiming that the planned revisions will achieve these goals then you need to be able to convince your colleagues. It's useful to review the current situation and test out your plans for improvement before committing yourself to major changes. You could:

- review a range of currently available resources throughout the school and see how effectively they are used;
- assess the degree to which selected commercially produced resources will meet the needs of your school;
- check to see the extent to which colleagues agree about the *exact* needs and requirements of the teaching staff, learning support staff, external agencies, etc.
- draw a diagram to show what the whole revision process will involve — use pictures, a time-line or an action-plan;
- use your diagrams, lists etc. to break the whole task down into smaller, more manageable stages and time scales;
- look at the proposed revision in terms of the degree of flexibility you can maintain;
- draw up plans that show how you will involve as many other people as possible, in different ways at different stages;
- monitor the revision process by matching what's done against your earlier objectives;
- accept differences of opinion as helpful, recognise that anxiety, frustration and feeling stuck are inevitable;
- bear in mind that postponing decisions can be a valuable strategy;
- draw up plans to show how colleagues will receive the support they ask for;
- draw up plans to ensure that you use the small amount of time available for collaborative work with colleagues as effectively as possible;
- prioritise the different parts of the revision process so you can maximise your effectiveness;
- discuss with colleagues the opportunities that exist for adopting new ways of working; e.g. in the teaching of mathematics, in organising and running meetings and the production of materials;

> There's a real danger that what is required in school is that children must:
> - work neatly all the time,
> - know the answer before starting,
> - get the maths right first time,
> - get it finished quickly.
>
> These are not the qualities that many mathematicians demonstrate.

- acknowledge your limitations and work creatively within them rather than ineffectively beyond them, drawing on support from colleagues and external expertise from the LEA and elsewhere.

What a revised scheme should aim to provide

1 **Revisions to the scheme should ensure that every child gets a diet of maths which is exciting, challenging, neither trivial nor overwhelming.** The National Curriculum offers opportunities for algebra, shape and space, data handling, probability, and measures as well as number. The maths diet for most children is richer now than it was ten years ago. A scheme of work needs to reflect this.

2 **It should ensure that children get an opportunity to work as mathematicians.** This is not as easy as it sounds because many people have strong stereotypes of what being a mathematician is like. Talking to adult mathematicians gives a picture of people who have ideas, can follow them up, often make mistakes, have to backtrack and try again, aren't always tidy, don't always find an answer, frequently get frustrated and get severely stuck on occasions, often achieve a breakthrough in their thinking when they've stopped working directly on the maths problem and are out walking the dog or cooking the children's tea. Many mathematicians also enjoy maths. The danger with primary school maths is that it can become quite unlike what adult mathematicians do.

Teachers are often very uncomfortable leaving children to stay with being stuck on a problem. Instead many teachers quickly find ways to smooth over the child's difficulties by changing the activity or by giving an explanation. Children need to be gently encouraged to stick with a problem rather than have the chance for intellectual struggle snatched away by teachers who find it uncomfortable when their children are in a situation where they do not know what to do for a while. The consequence of short-cutting the periods of genuine puzzlement is that children cannot develop as resilient learners. Obviously if the child is unhappy with being stuck then I'm not suggesting forcing the issue. But, too often, the opportunity to stay with the struggle is denied in favour of getting things finished. The result is that for many children maths remains something that is done **to** them in school and, in this scenario, the definition of the good mathematician becomes distorted into: someone who can work fast; who knows a lot; who answers questions correctly; who gets calculations right first time; and someone who gets good marks from the teacher. This definition fails to describe most of us and there is a real danger that the response of many children will continue to be: 'Maths? I hate it!'

3   **A scheme of work has got to offer simple advice about improving the way children are taught maths as well as indicating what is to be taught.** If a scheme of work doesn't support teachers then it isn't much use. Teachers vary in their need for support and guidance. A newly qualified teacher has quite different needs from a very experienced colleague. Meeting a range of needs within one scheme is not easy. A starting point is to talk to colleagues about their needs and what support is most likely to help them develop. They need to know that they are contributing to the school's overall aims; that they can do their own thing within clear guidelines and that if they use the scheme there is a real chance of improving the attainment of the children in their class.

4   **A scheme of work needs to be a working document from which teachers can make effective short-term plans, quickly, easily and with a minimum of copying or rewriting.** It needs to provide guidance on how to plan for continuity and progression of experience for children so that teachers can sustain children's progress. It should encourage a range of teaching and learning styles, and provide ideas and examples of activities. It should indicate the requirements of the National Curriculum and show how they are to be met.

Part four   Monitoring for quality

Chapter 17
Assessment

Exercising professional judgment

Assessment is the practice of making **professional judgments** about children's performance and achievement. It is sometimes confused with record-keeping which is quite a different issue. Effective record-keeping can only follow the sound professional judgments about assessment.

Assessment is a means to an end. The end is the achievement, by all pupils, of a degree of mathematical competence commensurate with their abilities and needs, and the development of appropriate attitudes to the subject.

(DES, 1985, p. 45)

The introduction of the National Curriculum has unfortunately blurred the distinction between assessment and record-keeping. Much of the political debate about these two important processes has sought to under-emphasise, even to undermine the teacher's professional role. Assessment has been recast, especially by politicians, primarily **as** record-keeping. This has made it possible to marginalise the role of the teacher in the assessment process. Instead of assessment being seen as the exercising of professional judgment, what has been promoted are 'scientific' claims about the objectivity and 'appropriateness' of SATs results.

There is a danger that assessment will be seen **only** as record-keeping. In such a climate, teacher assessment, both in its day-to-day, formative and informal roles, and in its more formal, summative, end of year and end of Key Stage role, is in danger of becoming the collection of numbers and the writing of reports. Thus one important aspect of teachers' professionalism is in danger of being marginalised. Instead of assessment as a professional responsibility, attempts have been made to recast assessment as mainly a bureaucratic process. It has been redefined by politicians in order to associate it with a supposed end-point of education, of assessing children's achievement. Assessment ceases to be a professional judgment exercised by individual teachers as part of their skill and their art. Instead, teachers are redefined as bureaucrats. Their job is not to exercise professional judgment but to use an imposed assessment scale to grade children's performance against a list of performance criteria issued by an authority which is external to the profession and to education.

Teachers must regain the assessment ground because assessment can only be a professional, judgmental act, performed by an expert. The reaffirmation of assessment as a core element in teachers' work is to reaffirm their unique status as professionals — no-one else has the professional training, expertise or opportunity to assess the day-to-day needs and achievements of children and produce an informed judgment of children's individual achievement.

The coordinator's role is crucial in this. Record-keeping needs to be seen as secondary to assessment and emerging from it. Record-keeping should follow, not drive, the teaching process and the exercising of professional judgment. It follows that all teachers need to be able to make confident and well-informed assessments of children's work in mathematics. Coordinators need to be clear about their own role and the wider professional role of teachers if they are to support teachers' professional development. It may be helpful to list the purposes of assessment and relate them to current practice in your own school.

The main purposes of assessment are:

1 To judge the value and appropriateness of the current lesson in relation to children's needs, abilities and interests.

2 To provide a means of monitoring the effectiveness of the teacher's role in mediating the children's learning and providing information about how best to modify subsequent teaching.

3 To maintain an accurate picture about where the children are in their thinking, their knowledge, skills and attitudes in relation to the various aspects of the curriculum.

4 To monitor children's varying ability to acquire and use knowledge and skills, and to demonstrate understanding.

5 To inform professional decisions during and after the lesson about the appropriateness of that lesson and the steps needed to ensure the appropriateness of the subsequent lesson.

6 To provide information derived from prior knowledge of the child and from classroom observation and use this information to mark children's work and 'level' selected items against attainment targets.

7 To judge children's overall performance and to match this to attainment targets using professional judgment to determine a 'best fit'.

8 To judge whether the children are progressing at a rate which is appropriate bearing in mind their previous attainment, and to respond to this professional decision by modifying what children are required to do.

9 To identify children's significant achievement and use the information as a basis for regular discussions about their performance, both with them and their parents or carers.

10 To provide a source of information about children's **significant achievement** so that this can be recorded and the information passed on to other interested parties.

Exploring the relationship between attainment and progress

Imagine having watched children working in the following three lessons. Below, in the table, are some brief notes you might have written. What reasonable responses could follow these observations?

Situation observed	Notes on attainment	Assessment of progress
A group of Y6 children of *high ability* who are lacking motivation, bored with some unchallenging tasks, ready to discuss big ideas but given little opportunity, working at some maths problems that are easy for them.	High for primary-aged children, because this group are Y6 and generally able to tackle work at level 5 or 6.	Poor, inadequate, because they are not being stretched. The work they are being given is level 3 or 4.
A mixed ability group of rising fives in an YR class. Two of the group are 4 years and 1 month. After 20 minutes of discussion and activity with the teacher involving cubes, they move back to their tables and working independently, they each construct all the combinations of cubes to make 4, then write independently an ordered list, 4+0=4, 3+1=4, etc. When talked to they clearly understand what they are doing.	High for Key Stage 1, some aspects of level 1 and some of level 2 at least.	Extremely good, the children understand what they are doing and the mathematics involved, the teacher's skill has created a learning environment where they are at the edge of what is possible for them.
A low attaining group of 8-year-olds with SEN working on additions and subtractions of money. With great effort, and real enthusiasm, they are mastering change to 50p but need careful guidance and support from the teacher who provides it very effectively.	Low — they are working at level 2 and cannot use decimal notation to represent amounts.	High. It is evident that they are acquiring understanding and learning new ideas, they are on the edge of their understanding and the teacher's organisation and manner have ensured maximum success and enjoyment and minimum error.

It is evident that the relationship between **attainment** and **progress** is complex and in practice is probably only understood by the teacher who is involved with the children as they work. A good knowledge of the children as people is needed if the teacher is to able to judge whether progress is appropriate in any given situation. When working on the development of the assessment process in school, the coordinator needs to take into account both *attainment* and *progress*, if there is to be any lasting development in the quality of maths education provided in the school.

The records that arise from the assessment process should be selective and should identify and describe individual children's **significant achievement**, rather than providing uncritical evidence of performance. Many schools still have a burdensome and over-elaborate record-keeping system. There is a lot of work to be done before we achieve a consensus about an adequate and simple record-keeping process that:

■ meets legal requirements;
■ demands the minimum time and effort from teachers;
■ ensures that the school collects and provides appropriate information for it to meet all its obligations.

Focusing on significant achievement allows the teacher to see the children's *progress* more clearly. Effective teaching ensures that some children will make huge leaps in a short space of time. Within the same class, one child may be making steady progress in most subjects but making big strides in mathematics. Another child may be making no progress in the acquisition of new ideas despite doing all the work set and having no difficulty with any of it. The effective teacher has to interpret this **range of performance** in relation to individual children and make appropriate changes to the teaching programme to ensure that children make the best progress possible. This professional knowledge means the teacher is in a position to make decisions about changing the nature and focus of lessons in order to raise educational standards in their classroom.

Record-keeping needs to support and serve the task of recording professional judgments. When it involves teachers in gathering irrelevant information, the record-keeping is inappropriate and inefficient. Where record-keeping is both irrelevant and onerous, the teacher is likely to miss the more important sources of evidence relating to the standards achieved. At the end of the day, if the teacher is collecting information that does not add to their professional knowledge of children's achievement then the information lacks professional value.

Tracking pupil's significant achievement

The assessment process must provide clear evidence of the attainment and progress of each child: both as an individual and as a member of various groups. Assessment and record-keeping must show how the quality of teaching is related to the quality of learning. This means each school needs to find an effective way of:

■ providing useful guidance to teachers about how to plan and carry out their assessments;
■ showing teachers how to record the results of various observations in ways that support children;
■ ensuring that assessment and record-keeping contribute directly to the raising of standards.

One school's approach to this was to meet together to discuss what they wanted and what manageable processes they could introduce to an already busy teaching load. The teachers wanted to track pupils in their class throughout the year and felt they could focus on a group of individual children each week if the associated record-keeping was simple enough. They decided only to record significant achievement and significant difficulties.

They took the important step of looking at the other methods of information gathering and recording already in place in the school. This helped them to see that the information they planned to collect in lessons was going to cover the same ground as the children's reports to parents, so they used the format of the child's report as their 'pupil tracking sheet'. Both sides are shown below in Figure 17.1. The tracking sheets are kept easily to hand in a folder in the classroom. A piece of card separates the sheets belonging to the 'target group' from those of the rest of the class. At the end of the week the target group's sheets are put to the back and the new group's sheets come to the top.

In their short-term planning, the staff include activities that are open-ended and which provide opportunities to show what children can do in relation to the work being covered in that curriculum subject. Not all subjects are being taught at once so evidence is being sought only for some subjects during any one period. The focus is on the core subjects, the children's attitudes to work and their social integration in the class. The teachers' short-term plans ensure they create some opportunity to observe and talk to the target group during selected activities. The notes made of significant

FRONT

Child's Name _____	
Class _____ Year Group _____	
Significant achievement and significant difficulties	
ENGLISH	Date
MATHS	
SCIENCE	
ATTITUDE AND BEHAVIOUR	

REVERSE

Academic Year: 199____/____	
Significant achievement and significant difficulties	
D & T IT PE	Date
ART MUSIC RE	
HISTORY GEOGRAPHY	
PARENTS' COMMENTS	

FIG 17.1
Children's report sheets also double as 'tracking records'

achievement and any major difficulties experienced by children in the group are dated. Teachers resist writing for the sake of it and do not record a pupil's performance if it is unremarkable — comments about this are better written in the child's book as a part of the normal marking process, or in any other notes the teachers might want to make for themselves. If another child not in the target group has a major difficulty or does something outstanding then of course they try to record that too.

What has emerged is the appearance of dated comments perhaps separated by a few weeks or months that show the children's development over time. 'Still having problems devising a fair test.' 3/11. 'Brilliant idea about devising a fair test for dropping paper helicopters — really got the hang of it!' 16/3. 'Not ready to tackle degrees in a right angle — just can't see what the numbers represent. Complete blank.' 27/09 'Able to describe angle as measure of turn — gave good explanation, led the group confidently'. 15/11.

The bonus, when reports have to be written for parents, is that much of information is already recorded, and in a format that can be easily transferred to a neat final copy. Similarly, information about achievement — parents' main concern — is also clearly organised in a useful format that allows the teacher to recall significant moments in the child's experience and give parents specific examples when they meet at a parents' meeting.

When Penny, the school's deputy discussed this work with us she made it clear that teachers had thought hard about whether it was achievable. They decided to trial it and then review it after one whole year. When this method of tracking was discussed with other teachers on the course, several thought that this style of working wouldn't fit their classroom routine. Some began devising a group sheet that met their needs. They were less concerned about making links with the school report. They were more interested in linking the recording of significant achievement to their weekly planning sheets for which they used two A3 layouts one for core and the other for foundation subjects. The result of their work is the short-term planning sheet on shown on p. 187.

Their planning sheet provides enough space for groups of children to be identified along with the related activities. The boxes on the reverse side were made visible by being folded back to cover the RESOURCES section on the front. So, when being used to record assessments, the front section describing the activities was visible along with the folded-over boxes where teachers could write a group comment, only referring to individual children when necessary. These are just two possible, tried-and-tested ways of recording children's significant achievement.

Target setting

Many schools have found that sharing the assessment process with the children has brought about considerable improvement in children's performance. The process might be developed as follows:

1 During a lesson, the teacher talks briefly to a group and tells individual children about things they are doing well and things they could improve on. The children are asked to select **one specific thing** that they want to improve. They might choose: smaller writing, trying to stop reversing their letters and numerals, speed of working, gossiping less, using the number line to check mental work, etc. The teacher writes the child's exact words onto a small piece of card which fits inside their workbook. Every time the child starts some mathematics, the card is brought out and is propped up in front of them where the child and teacher can both see it.

2 As the child works, the teacher congratulates good effort, reminds them of their target, and fairly soon, when progress has been made, the card can be discarded and other one can be written to replace it. If the child fails to be careful then the teacher can remind them by referring to the card. After a short while of focusing on maths, the child and teacher may want to have a rest or move onto another curriculum area. The teacher may want to encourage just one group of children at a time, for a week or two, then move to another group.

Target groups

Identifying target groups of children for observation is part of the cycle of *planning, teaching* and *evaluating* outlined as follows. In a large class where there are more than twenty children, it is inappropriate to attempt to make observations of all the children during a single lesson. Teachers can observe general progress but can only make detailed assessments of a small target group. What follows is one way of doing this.

1 The teacher identifies a target group of children each week.
2 For each maths lesson, the teacher writes a brief but specific phrase in the weekly planning sheet about what the target group of children will be able to do by the end of the lesson, assuming the lesson has been appropriate for them: e.g. *identify halves and quarters in different situations.*
3 At the start of the lesson the children are told what they will be able to do by the end of the lesson — they will then know for themselves whether they have had a good lesson and worked well.
4 Near the end of the lesson, during a whole-class plenary session, the teacher discusses with the children whether they are able to do what was wanted. This session includes asking the children to demonstrate what they know and what they can do.
5 The teacher tells the children how well they've done in terms of their new-found knowledge and skills.
6 The children's work is collected (some marking may well have been done with the children during the lesson). The teacher assesses the children's performance and marks their work.
7 The teacher briefly reviews the plans for the next lesson based on what the curriculum suggests should come next, on the teacher's own effectiveness, **and also** on what the children have **achieved** in relation to the **progress** the teacher thinks they are capable of making.

The teacher can keep a dated note of the children's targets and can keep a record of their progress towards them. This is useful material to use when children select work to be included in their record of achievement because it provides the child with their own criteria for selection. It is also useful material to use at parents' evenings because it is specific to individual children and is focused on:

- what the child can do;
- how the child has improved.

Improving teaching and learning

The three major purposes of assessment are to:
- Promote the quality of teaching.
- Promote the quality of learning and raise children's achievement to the highest levels possible.
- To provide information to the children, their parents and to others as appropriate.

The effective use of assessment to inform future planning has a significant effect on the quality of teaching. It enables the teacher to adjust the future lessons that form the future programme of activities. As a result of changes to future teaching based on assessment of current work, the teacher is more likely to meet the needs of the children. When assessment informs future planning, children of different abilities are more likely to be appropriately challenged.

Diagnostic, and formative assessment provide children with valuable information about their current performance and this has a significant effect on the quality of learning. Diagnostic assessment of children's mistakes and misunderstanding is crucial in helping them to improve current strategies, to overcome difficulties and to develop secure methods of working. Formative assessment carried out part way through a teaching programme allows both the children and the teacher to inform and modify their work. Children benefit from being told whether they are meeting the targets set, and teachers can modify their teaching to help children more easily meet these targets.

Guided by the teacher, the children can set some of their own targets and monitor their own performance. Self assessment, where children discuss and record their own achievements has a powerful effect on their motivation. It also gives them greater insight into their own learning styles and reinforces the idea that they must take responsibility for their own learning. It ensures a greater independence from the teacher and encourages greater robustness. Children who set and work towards their own targets are less likely to give up when they face difficulties.

Summative assessment is useful for providing evidence of achievement. It forms the basis of formal recording and reporting. When schools have to set their own targets, as proposed in the 1997 Education Act, summative assessment will provide evidence of whether the school's targets have been met.

Part five Resources for learning

Chapter 18   Managing resources

Human resources

The most valuable resource children have available other than their own intellect are the adults who work with them. In education we rarely practice what we preach about caring for others. We generally do not take enough care of the human resources that are needed to make schools work.

The newly appointed coordinator needs to quickly acquire a whole school viewpoint and begin to take responsibility for mathematics beyond their own classroom. Getting a clear picture of what's 'going on' is a skilful process and includes looking at the human resources that are potentially available. Success is likely to be best achieved when everyone in the school sees the need for coordinators to have a whole school viewpoint and are confident in talking about their strengths and their anxieties where teaching maths is concerned. Most of us do not teach maths equally effectively across the whole subject and it's refreshing to know that this is normal and we're not alone. Thought about positively — we can consider ourselves as always ripe for development.

Ideas can be shared and, in many schools, the ideas offered by individual teachers to their children spawn other

FIG 18.1
Auditing use of resources in
school

Think about an activity you like using with your children	Comments below please
What I call the activity. The resources I use. Which topics the activity supports.	
What I need to get myself organised.	
What I and the children talk about.	
What I expect the children to already know.	
What I expect the children to be able to do.	
What I do to support the children as they work.	
How I judge the outcomes.	
Where I go next.	

activities with other age groups throughout the school. For example, coordinators can prepare a questionnaire like that shown in Figure 18.1, which asks teachers to comment on a resource they like using. Teachers can file completed sheets in the staff room under headings organised by the coordinator. The sheets can accumulate rapidly and they provide a useful way of encouraging teachers to use and adapt each other's ideas. There is a lot of professional experience within any school and staff are a valuable source of ideas that will support professional development.

Courses

There is always a delicate balance between the professional needs of individual colleagues and the needs of the school. There simply isn't enough money around to meet the demand for inservice courses. A balance has to be struck between school development and the professional development of individuals. This balance is most appropriately achieved through the School Development Plan. The planning cycle should start by considering matters a year or more in advance. This allows the needs of the school and the individuals to be balanced. Needs have to be met through a programme of planned action which is recorded in the SDP. Planning for courses can sometimes be difficult, especially when it is not known what LEA, GEST or other locally provided courses may be offered in the future. Each proposed plan of action needs to be costed wherever possible. If targets are clear and people are not coerced, then there are three valuable stages to ensuring that both the school and the individual gets good value for money from the course.

1 Before the course starts, what preparation can teachers make? What reading, reflection, thinking and talking will best prepare someone to get the most out of an inevitably brief course? How can they be supported? How will they know what the school's needs are? How can the desire for improvement be kept in check so that quality rather than quantity is likely to emerge from a course? What is known about the people running the course? Will the course be adapted to meet needs? How will course leaders know what's required?

2 During the course, most people are too ambitious and try to do too much. Sometimes they are disappointed because they don't get as much done as they hoped (and other people expect). Some feel guilty that they have an opportunity to be away from school — feeling guilty doesn't always lead to creative thinking so try to prevent this. Some courses are about collecting ideas and tips and this is perfectly legitimate. Others are about taking stock, reviewing current thinking. There is much discussion at the moment about the value of developing more whole class teaching. This issue deserves careful consideration.

It's important to know whether the course is offering what you expect and need.

3 After the course, it's very easy to get swallowed up in the day-to-day work of class teaching and not have time to think about what was learned on the course. Expensive but potentially cost-effective, is the decision to identify in the SDP to pay for some non-contact time after a course. Even if the course has only been half a day, it's possible that by providing a further half-day classroom release, the ideas developed on a course can be made to benefit the school more effectively.

Material resources auditing

1 One way of starting to think about provision is to walk through the school looking at all the maths equipment in terms of availability (does everyone have equal access), quality and quantity, accessibility to adults and children. In some schools just carrying out this exercise is difficult because over the years, some teachers may have acquired resources that they regard 'theirs'; they may not tell you what they've got and certainly won't take kindly to you removing it from their classroom and putting it in a central area.

2 You could look at children's work on display, children's books, scheme books, etc. and assess what resources are used each week, each term. Why do some teachers make heavy use of some items — have they got good ideas to share? Why do some pieces of equipment rarely get used — do people know the equipment exists, can they use it confidently? Is there equipment demanded by the school scheme but not available?

3 You could identify specific mathematics topics taught during the year and match them to the required resources to see if there are sufficient available to teach the topics in the relevant age groups. This will help with the monitoring and development of the medium-term planning.

4 There should be an inventory of mathematics resources and stock. You could use the inventory to check the items listed against what is found. A copy of the inventory

Class	Reasons for keeping the current arrangements for maths resources	Reasons for changing current arrangements	Notes: Specific things that we lack. Things that we need to be addressing, e.g. ways of using equipment
1			
2			

FIG 18.2
Audit form for material resources

could then be sent to each class teacher so they can see what is potentially available for them to use.

5 You could give everyone a simple form to fill in and return (see Figure 18.2), to remind them of their responsibilities for using, returning and maintaining resources, and to encourage them to be part of the auditing process.

As a result of an audit of physical resources you should be able to answer some basic questions.

Are there enough resources — are they in good enough condition?

Can resources be made more easily available by redistribution, by an amnesty where everyone owns up to what they've got, by a change in the timing when people teach certain topics — everyone teaching *capacity* at the same time means high demand of some resources and a lot of other equipment under-used during the same period.

Are any areas of maths under-resourced?

This may be due to previous purchasing arrangements, or high wear and tear, bad storage, lack of familiarity with a curriculum area — but buying new resources is the last thing to do. Check first why the range of resources has left an area or a topic poorly equipped. Has equipment been loaned or stored? Do you have to buy what you need? Patterned fabrics, carpet tiles, wallpaper samples, conkers, rice, pasta, knitted toys, photographs, all have a place in the teaching of

217

maths. Many of them can be acquired and added to stock at no extra financial cost.

Equality and equal access

Are some children disadvantaged because they cannot use the equipment that's available? Is some equipment too heavy or too large for young children, not suitable for children in wheelchairs or with poor vision. Do teachers have equal access or does some of it 'belong' to one teacher who is reluctant to loan it out. Is a newly created class taken by the NQT properly stocked or have they been given everyone else's leftovers?

Do people know how to use the equipment?

This is a useful opportunity to get more experienced members of staff to talk about the way they teach maths. You could run an after-school session with a focus on one type of resource and ask everybody to contribute: Bring three good starting points for using squared paper with 5-year-olds.

Catalogues lists and inventories

Are lists and catalogues of the school's mathematics resources up-to-date and easily accessible?2 Can people tell at a glance what is available before they ask you to buy something the school has already got?

Are the current storage arrangements suiting everyone?

Have you got a compromise that works? Can something be done to improve matters? Have you included audio-visual aids, cassette storage for TV and radio programmes, posters, the published scheme material?

It is essential for items to be accessible and the most likely compromise in many schools is to have a basic classroom stock with more expensive and less frequently used equipment stored centrally. Ideally, the regularly used items stored in classrooms will be clearly labelled and positioned so that children can do most of the getting out and putting away. Older children can become involved in designing classroom layouts, making labels and planning rotas of who is to be responsible. Even the youngest children can contribute to discussions about the best places to store equipment in terms of safety, accessibility and ease of distribution in the classroom. Newly arrived members of staff need a basic set of equipment in their room that's appropriate for the age group they are teaching. In-service sessions can be used to look at different ways in which resources are used.

Can children select appropriate resources?
One of the expectations in the *using and applying* Programme of Study is that children should be able to show an increasing awareness of the most appropriate resources to use when carrying out work. This presupposes:
- they are familiar and confident with using a range of different equipment and have the skills to use it;
- that there are regular opportunities for children to respond to questions that expect children to make a choice or a selection. This can be a guided choice on occasions, where the teacher puts out two or three examples and asks the children to choose and say why they've chosen.

Developing the use of resources

How someone uses Cuisenaire rods, calculators or graph paper is intimately bound up in their own knowledge and understanding of maths, and the styles of teaching they adopt. The way in which computers are used, and the way in which ideas about angles are taught, should be different throughout the school. Resources should be used in different ways at different times in classrooms as children progress in their thinking.

Staff development sessions will steadily raise the quality of use of resources, through demonstration but also through discussion, particularly if the sessions focus on what mathematical thinking we want to develop through the use of a particular piece of equipment. You may want to include learning support staff, volunteers and parents in these sessions because classroom helpers often use resources when they work closely alongside individual children.

It's not what you do it's the way that you do it — colleagues need to know the best questions and activities to use to promote mathematical thinking. Structured apparatus is a particularly important teaching resource. When used effectively structured apparatus supports learning by:

- providing a framework for thinking and for the exploration of ideas;
- providing a focus for discussion;
- allowing the teacher to pose complex and challenging questions;
- allowing children to work with visual representations of mathematical structures;
- illustrating a way of thinking mathematically;
- acting as an aide-memoire, by freeing up our memory (one of our weakest faculties) leaving more opportunity for creative thinking;
- allowing visual comparison of results to problems and investigations, so that children can literally 'see what they're doing';
- allowing children to physically model problems;
- allowing time for thinking as resources are manipulated.

It's vital that teachers are familiar with what resources can offer in terms of **scaffolding** children's thinking. Part of this pedagogical knowledge emerges when one learns the most useful instructions to give and the most effective questions to pose when using resources. This requires inservice work and support and assumes that coordinators are familiar with the use of resources and know what teacher talk is most effective.

Budgeting

Being responsible for maths means that you really need to be the person responsible for managing the expenditure of the maths budget. Of course colleagues should have a say in what is bought, but it is not good financial management to let colleagues spend a sum of money on any maths equipment they want and hope that as a result you will be able to cover the teaching of mathematics effectively throughout the school. Purchases have to be managed so that a little money goes as far as you can stretch it. That means having a clear picture of what is needed for replacement and maintenance and then having a priority list for development of resources.

A whole school approach to planning as a staff and the careful use of the school's long-term planning guides allows maths topics to be planned throughout the school so that teachers do not all need the same equipment at the same time. By making slight changes to the order in which topics are taught you can reduce demand on equipment and save hundreds of pounds. In stead of duplicating resources you can spend money on urgently needed software or other new equipment.

Efficient use of the budget is achieved when you have acquired just enough equipment and resources for them to be fully used most of the time. Budget responsibility can sometimes be difficult to acquire. If you need support in introducing this idea then it's likely that other coordinators will be facing the same situation as you are. This would suggest that this is a whole school issue which could be tackled by the deputy head or through the help of a local authority adviser.

Computer resources

The computer resources you have available should support all the Programmes of Study and allow teachers to achieve specific goals. This means the best arrangements for storing software might be by Programme of Study. Along with the software, you could include (in a clear plastic envelope), a sheet outlining how the particular Programme of Study is supported. (See Figure 18.3 for an example).

Programme of Study	Key Stage 1 detail	Key Stage 2 detail
Using and applying	4. Developing mathematical reasoning. b. Ask questions including *'What would happen if?'* and *'Why'* e.g. *considering the behaviour of a programmable toy.*	3. Communicating mathematically b. use mathematical forms of communication, including diagrams, tables, graphs and computer printouts.
Number and algebra	1. pupils should be given opportunities to: f. use computer software including a database	1. Pupils should be given opportunities to: b. use calculators, computers and a range of other resources as tools for exploring number structure and to enable work with realistic data
Shape space and measures	1. Pupils should be given opportunities to: b. use IT devices, e.g. programmable toys, *turtle graphics packages.* Understanding and using properties of position and movement b. understand angle as a measure of turn and recognise quarter-turns, e.g. giving instructions for rotating a programmable toy; recognise right angles.	1. Pupils should be given opportunities to: c. use computers to create and transform shapes.
Handling data		1. Pupils should be given opportunities to: c. use computers as a source of interesting data, and as a tool for representing data. 2. Collecting, representing and interpreting data. b. collect and represent discrete data appropriately using graphs and diagrams, including block graphs, pictograms and line graphs; interpret a wider range of graphs and diagrams that represent data, including pie charts, using a computer where appropriate.

FIG 18.3
References to IT in the mathematics National Curriculum

Computer Software

There is some exciting software now available for teaching and learning mathematics. What follows is a small selection that schools have found useful. As always, there is considerable variation in quality and it is important to try software out before purchasing.

Some of the old BBC software still provides some useful teaching and learning opportunities.

Software title and publisher	PC platform CDrom	Acorn disc based	PC disc based	First launched
Mathematics Dictionary, by Polydron International for Key Stage 2	✓			1997
Fun School Maths 7–11, by Europa Press	✓			1997
Tizzy's Toybox, by Sherston for young children	✓			1997
The Logical Journey of the Zoombinis by Broderbund	✓			1996
Maths Workshop, by Broderbund for ages 6–10	✓			1995
Strategy Games of the World, by Iona/Edmark for KS 2	✓			1995
SIM Life by Maxis	✓			1995
SIM Earth by Maxis	✓			1995
Elf Tales (Elf Magic and Elf King) by Sherston for KS1		✓		1996
Table Aliens Sherston		✓		1996
Number Genie Computer Tutorials		✓		1996
Clockwise by 4mation		✓		1995
First LOGO by Longman Logotron for KS 1		✓		1993
Maths Circus by 4mation mainly for KS2 with some KS1 activities		✓		1993
Graph IT Sherston		✓		1992
Ginn Mathematics Level 2 Software Ginn & Co Ltd.			✓	1997
Super Window Box by Research Machines Ltd. A collection of programs including word processing and spread sheet together with several Cd roms			✓	1997

Old Software primary mathematics on the BBC platform

Teddy Bear's Picnic by Sherston

Connections by Sherston

Information Handling Pack by NCET

Problem Solving Pack by NCET

Chapter 19

Useful contacts

There are a number of associations and centres that supply information, run conferences and meetings, and publish ideas and resources for the teaching and learning of mathematics. Local authorities, local colleges and universities offer courses for coordinators.

Addresses

Association of Teachers of Mathematics (ATM), 7 Shaftesbury Street, Derby DE3 8YB

AUCBE, Endymion Road, Hatfield, Herts AL11 8AU

Be A Mathematician (BEAM), Barnsbury Complex, Offord Road, London N1 1QH

Brøderbund Software, Unit A, Sovereign Park, Brenda Road, Hartlepool, Cleveland, TS25 1NN

Centre for Mathematics Education, Open University, Walton Hall, Milton Keynes MK7 6AA

Cambridge Software House (CSH), The Town Hall, St Ives, Huntingdon, Cambridge PE17 4AL

ESM, Duke Street, Wisbech, Cambridgeshire PE13 2AE

Europa Press, Europa House, Adlington Park, Macclesfield, SK10 4NP

Fernleaf Educational Software, Fernleaf House, 31, Old Road West, Gravesend, Kent DA11 0LH

Fossil Hall, Boars Tye Road, Silver End, Witham, Essex MC8 3QA

4mation Educational Software, Linden Lea, Rock Park, Barnstaple, Devon EX32 9QA

Ginn & Co. Prebendal House, Parson's Fee, Aylesbury, Buckinghamshire HP20 2QZ

ILECC, Supplies Department, John Ruskin Street, London SE5 0PQ

ITSCST, Tunstall Court, Gore Court Road, Sittingbourne, Kent ME10 1QL

Logotron Ltd., Dales Brewery, Gwydir Street, Cambridge CB1 2LJ

MAPE, Newman College, Bartley Green, Birmingham B32 3NT

MESU/NCET (Software Orders), Hoddle, Doyle and Meadows, Old Mead Road, Elsingham, Bishop Stortford, Herts CM2 6JN

Mathematical Association (MA), 259, London Road, Leicester LE2 8BE

Northamptonshire Computer Education Centre, Barry Road, Northampton NN1 5JS

Northern Micromedia, Resources Centre, Coach Lane Campus, Newcastle upon Tyne NE7 7XA

Oxfordshire County Council, Computer Education Unit, Wheatley Centre, Littleworth Road, Wheatley, Oxon OX9 1PH

Polydron International, Kemble, Cirencester, Gloucestershire, GL7 6BA

Swallow Systems, 32 High Street, High Wycombe, Bucks HP1 2AQ

Selective Software, 64 Brookes Road, Street, Somerset BA16 0PP

Shell Centre for Mathematical Education, University of Nottingham, Nottingham NG7 2RD

Sherston Software, Angel House, Sherston, Malmesbury, Wiltshire, SN16 0LH

Maths Centre activity books, (*Bounce to it*, *Leap to it*, etc.) Manchester Metropolitan University, Didsbury, Manchester

Valiant Technology Ltd., Gulf House, 370 York Road, Wandsworth, London SW18 1SP

World Wide Web

Ask Dr. Math	http://forum.swarthmore.edu/dr.math/drmath.elem.html
ATM	http://acorn.educ.nottingham.ac.uk//SchEd/pages/atm
Big Sky Lesson Plans	http://forum.swarthmore.edu/~steve/steve/bigsky.elem.html
Freudenthal Institute	http://www.fi.ruu.nl
Fun with numbers	http://www.mind.net/xethyr/numbers/index.html
Maths Archives	http://archives.math.utk.edu/index#contents
On-line maths directory	http://www.mathpro.com/math/glossary/glossary.html
UK Schools: maths resources	http://www.liv.ac.uk/~evansjon/maths/menu.html

Suggested reading

Journals

Mathematics Teaching, Derby: Association of Teachers of Mathematics.
Mathematics in Schools, Mathematical Association.
Primary Maths + Science, The Questions Publishing Company, 27 Frederick Street, Birmingham B1 3HH

General books

ALEXANDER, R. (1992) *Policy and Practice in Primary Education*, London: Routledge.
ANGHILERI, J. (ed) (1995) *Children's Mathematical Thinking in the Primary Years: Perspectives on Children's Learning*, London: Cassell.
ATKINSON, S. (1996) *Developing a Scheme of Work for Primary Mathematics*, London: Hodder & Stoughton.
BALL, G. (1990) *Talking and Learning*, Oxford, Blackwell.
BIRD, M. (1991) *Mathematics for Young Children*, London: Routledge.
BLINKO, J. and SLATER, A. (1996) *Teaching Measures*, London: Hodder & Stoughton.

BRISSENDEN, T. (1988) *Talking about Mathematics*, Oxford: Blackwell.

BURTON, L. (1984) *Thinking Things Through: Problem Solving in Mathematics*, Oxford: Blackwell.

BURTON, L. (ed) (1986) *Girls into Maths Can Go*, London: Holt Rinehart & Winston.

CENTRE FOR MATHEMATICS EDUCATION, (1990) *Supporting Primary Mathematics: Working with Colleagues*, Milton Keynes: Open University.

CLARKE, S. and ATKINSON, S. (1996) *Tracking Significant Achievement in Primary Maths*, London: Hodder & Stoughton.

CLEMSON, D. and CLEMSON, W. (1994) *Mathematics in the Early Years*, London: Routledge.

DES (1985) *Mathematics from 5 to 16*, Curriculum Matters 3: an HMI series, London: HMSO.

DICKSON, L., BROWN, M. and GIBSON, O. (1992) *Children learning mathematics: A Teacher's Guide to Recent Research*, 2nd Edition, London: Cassell.

DRUMMOND, M. J. (1993) *Assessing Children's Learning*, London: Fulton.

GRAHAM, N. and BLINKO, J. (1991) *Zero to Ninety Nine: Problem Solving on a Hundred Square*, Claire Publications.

HAYLOCK, D. (1995) *Mathematics Explained for Primary Teachers*, London: Paul Chapman Publishing.

HUGHES, M., WIKELEY, F. and NASH, T. (1994) 'Parents and their children's schools', in POLLARD, A. (ed) *Readings for Reflective Teaching in the Primary School*, London: Cassell.

ILEA (1988) *Mathematics in ILEA Primary Schools Part 1, A Handbook for Teachers, and Part 2, A Handbook for Coordinators*, London: ILEA.

LEWIS, A. (1996) *Discovering Mathematics with 4 to 7 Year Olds*, London: Hodder & Stoughton.

MERTTENS, R. and VASS, J. (1990) *Sharing Maths Cultures: IMPACT, Inventing Maths for Parents and Children and Teachers*, London: Falmer Press.

MERTTENS, R. and BROWN T. (1997) '*Number operations and procedures*', in MERTTENS, R. (ed) *Teaching Numeracy*, London: Scholastic Publications.

PIMM, D. and LOVE, E. (eds) (1991) *Teaching and Learning School Mathematics*, London: Hodder & Stoughton.

PIMM, D. (ed) (1988) *Mathematics, Teachers and Children*, London: Hodder & Stoughton and Open University.

STRAKER, A. (1993) *Talking Points in Mathematics*, Cambridge: Cambridge University Press.

STRAKER, A. and GOVIER, H. (1997) *Children Using Computers*: (2nd edition), Oxford: Nash Pollock Publishing.

ZASLAVSKY, C. (1973) *Africa Counts*, Lawrence Hill.

ZASLAVSKY, C. (1980) *Count on Your Fingers African Style*, T Y Crowell (available from Jonathan Press).

ZASLAVSKY, C. (1996) *Multicultural Math Classroom*, London: Heinemann.

Activity books

ATM (1991) *Exploring maths with younger children*, Derby: Association of Teachers of Mathematics.

ATM (1993) *P'raps, p'raps not . . .* , Derby: Association of Teachers of Mathematics.

ATM (1992) *Ten Squared*, Derby: Association of Teachers of Mathematics.

BBC EARLY *Years* (monthly magazine) *Learning is fun*, BBC in association with BBC Education.

EBBUTT, S. and MOSLEY, F. (1996) *Exploring shape and space*, London: BEAM.

IMPACT MATHS ACTIVITIES (1994) *Measuring*. London: Scholastic Publications.

LANGDON, N. and SNAPE, C. (1984) *A Way with Maths*, Cambridge: Cambridge University Press.

Dictionaries and reference

CAMBRIDGE UNIVERSITY PRESS (1994) *Mathswords: A Book for Mathematics*, Cambridge: Cambridge University Press.

HORRIL, P. (1986) *Maths A–Z*, Harlow: Longman.

KLAEBE, K. (1986) *HBJ: Dictionary of Mathmatics*, London: Harcourt, Brace Jovanovich.

WELLS, D. (1986) *The Penguin Dictionary of curious and interesting numbers*, London: Penguin.

References

ASKEW, M. (1995) *Number at Key Stage 1: Core Materials for Teaching and Assessing Number and Algebra*, London: BEAM.

ASKEW, M. (1995) *Number at Key Stage 2: Core Materials for Teaching and Assessing Number and Algebra*, London: BEAM.

BONNETT, M. (1995) 'Teaching thinking, and the sanctity of content', *Journal of Philosophy of Education*, Vol. **29**, No. 3.

BRUNER, J. (1996) *The Culture of Education*, Harvard: Harvard University Press.

CLAXTON, G. (1989) *Being a Teacher: A Positive Approach to Change and Stress*, London: Cassell.

CLAXTON, G. (1997) *Hare Brain, Tortoise Mind: Why Intelligence Increases When You Think Less*, London: Fourth Estate.

CROLL, P. (ed) (1996) *Teachers, Pupils and Primary Schooling: Continuity and Change*, London: Cassell.

DAVIS, J. (1990) *Algebra: Supporting Primary Mathematics PM649*, Milton Keynes: Centre for Mathematics Education, Open University.

DES (1982) *Mathematics Counts* (Cockcroft Report), London: HMSO.

DES (1985) *Mathematics 5–16 Matters for Discussion Series*, HMSO.

DONALDSON, M. (1978) *Children's Minds*, London: Fontana.

DONALDSON, M. (1992) *Human Minds*, London: Penguin.

DUNCAN, A. (1992) *What Primary Teachers should know about Maths*, London: Hodder & Stoughton.

EDUCATION WHITE PAPER (1992) *Choice and Diversity: A New Framework for Schools*, London: HMSO.

ERNEST, P. (ed) (1994) *Constructing Mathematical Knowledge: Epistemology and Mathematical Education*, London: Falmer Press.

FEUERSTEIN, R. (1983) *Instrumental Enrichment*, University Park Press.

FISHER, R. (1990) *Teaching Children to Think*, London: Blackwell.

GARDNER, H. (1993) *Frames of Mind: The Theory of Multiple Intelligences*, 2nd Edition, London: Fontana.

GARDNER, H. (1993) *The Unschooled Mind: How Children Think and How Schools Should Teach*, London: Fontana.

GATTEGNO, C. (1971) *What We Owe Children: The Subordination of Teaching to Learning*, London: Routledge & Kegan Paul.

HARRIS, S. et al. (1997) *Third International Maths and Science Study*, (*TIMSS*) London: NFER.

HOPKINS, C. et al. (1996) *Mathematics in the Primary School: A Sense of Perspective*, London: David Fulton.

HUGHES, M. (1984) *Children and Number*, London: Blackwell.

ILEA (1988) *Mathematics in ILEA Primary Schools, Part 1: Children and Mathematics — A Handbook for Teachers*, London: Harcourt Brace Jovanovitch.

ILEA (1988) *Mathematics in ILEA Primary Schools, Part 2: A Handbook for the Mathematics Coordinator*, London: Harcourt Brace Jovanovitch.

JOYCE, B. et al. (1997) *Models of Learning: Tools for Teaching*, Buckingham: Open University Press.

KRUTETSKI, V. A. (1976) *The Psychology of Mathematical Abilities in Schoolchildren*, Chicago: University of Chicago Press.

LAAR, B. (1997) *The TES Guide to Surviving School Inspection*, London: Butterworth Heinemann.

LAING, R. D. (1970) *Knots*, London: Penguin.

LEWIS, A. (1996) *Discovering Maths with 4 to 7 Year Olds*, London: Hodder & Stoughton.

MACNAMARA, A. (1995) 'Mathematics', in ANNING, A. (ed) *A National Curriculum for the Early Years*, Milton Keynes: Open University Press.

MATHEMATICAL ASSOCIATION (1987) *Sharing Mathematics with Parents: Planning School-based Events*, Cheltenham: Stanley Thorne.

McCARTHY, B. (1987) *The 4MAT System*, EXCEL Barrington III.

MERTTENS, R. and VASS, J. (1993) *Partnership in Maths: Parents and Schools, The IMPACT Project*, London: Falmer Press.

MERTTENS, R. (ed) (1997) *Teaching Numeracy*, Scholastic Publications.

MERTTENS, R. et al. (1997) *Abacus Mathematics*, London: Ginn.

NELSON MATHEMATICS, Nelson Publishing Company, London: Nelson.

OFSTED (Office for Standards in Education), (1994) *Science and Mathematics in Schools*, London: HMSO.

PIMM, D. (1987) *Speaking Mathematically*, London: Routledge.

PLUNKETT, S. (1979) 'Decomposition and all that rot', *in Mathematics in Schools*, Mathematical Association.

POSTMAN, N. and WEINGARTNER, C. (1973) *Teaching as a Subversive Activity*, London: Penguin, Harmondsworth.

PrIME PROJECT: (1991) *Calculators, Children and Mathematics*, published for National Curriculum Council, *CAN (The Calculator-Aware Number Curriculum)*, Hemel Hempstead: Simon & Schuster.

PrIME (1992) *Children, Mathematics and Learning*, published for National Curriculum Council by Simon & Schuster.

REYNOLDS, D. and FARRELL, S. (1996) *Worlds Apart?: A Review of International Surveys of Educational Achievement Involving England*, London: OFSTED.

SCAA (1995) *Consistency in Teacher Assessment: Exemplification of Standards at Key Stages 1 and 2*, York: SCAA.

SHARRON, H. (1994) *Changing Children's Minds*, Sharron Publishing.

WINNICOTT, D. (1986) *Home Is Where We Start From: Essays by a Psychoanalyst*, London: Penguin.

'A Guide to the National Numeracy Project', *Primary Maths & Science, September 1997*, Birmingham: Questions Publishing Company.

Index

ORDER FORM

Post: *Customer Services Department, Falmer Press, Rankine Road, Basingstoke, Hampshire, RG24 8PR*
Tel: *(01256) 813000* **Fax**: *(01256) 479438*
E-mail: *book.orders@tandf.co.uk*

10% DISCOUNT AND FREE P&P FOR SCHOOLS OR INDIVIDUALS ORDERING THE COMPLETE SET ORDER YOUR SET NOW. WITH CREDIT CARD PAYMENTS, YOU WON'T BE CHARGED TILL DESPATCH.

TITLE	DUE	ISBN	PRICE	QTY
SUBJECT LEADERS' HANDBOOKS SET		**(RRP £207.20)**	**£185.00**	
Coordinating Science	2/98	0 7507 0688 0	£12.95	
Coordinating Design and Technology	2/98	0 7507 0689 9	£12.95	
Coordinating Maths	2/98	0 7507 0687 2	£12.95	
Coordinating Physical Education	2/98	0 7507 0693 7	£12.95	
Coordinating History	2/98	0 7507 0691 0	£12.95	
Coordinating Music	2/98	0 7507 0694 5	£12.95	
Coordinating Geography	2/98	0 7507 0692 9	£12.95	
Coordinating English at Key Stage 1	4/98	0 7507 0685 6	£12.95	
Coordinating English at Key Stage 2	4/98	0 7507 0686 4	£12.95	
Coordinating IT	4/98	0 7507 0690 2	£12.95	
Coordinating Art	4/98	0 7507 0695 3	£12.95	
Coordinating Religious Education	Late 98	0 7507 0613 9	£12.95	
Management Skills for SEN Coordinators	Late 98	0 7507 0697 X	£12.95	
Building a Whole School Assessment Policy	Late 98	0 7507 0698 8	£12.95	
Curriculum Coordinator and OFSTED Inspection	Late 98	0 7507 0699 6	£12.95	
Coordinating Curriculum in Smaller Primary School	Late 98	0 7507 0700 3	£12.95	

Value of Books	
P&P*	
Total	

*Please add p&p
orders up to £25   *10%*
orders from £25 to £50   *5%*
orders over £50   *free*

I wish to pay by:

❑ Cheque *(Pay Falmer Press)*

❑ Pro-forma invoice

❑ Credit Card *(Mastercard / Visa / AmEx)*

Card Number _____   *Expiry Date* _____

Signature _____

Name _____ *Title/Position* _____

School _____

Address _____

Postcode _____ *Country* _____

Tel no. _____ *Fax* _____

E-mail _____

❑ If you do not wish to receive further promotional information from the Taylor&Francis Group, please tick box.
All prices are correct at time of going to print but may change without notice

Ref: 1197BFSLAD